SAMUEL BECKETT'S REAL SILENCE

Hélène L. Baldwin

The Pennsylvania State University Press
University Park and London

Matri meae filiaeque

Works by Samuel Beckett are quoted by permission of Grove Press, Inc.

Library of Congress Cataloging in Publication Data

Baldwin, Helene Louise, 1920,
Samuel Beckett's real silence.
Includes bibliography and index.
1.Beckett, Samuel, 1906–
--Criticism and interpretation. I. Title.
PQ2603.E378Z55   848'.91409   80–21465
ISBN 0-271-00301-4

Contents

Preface

This study began in a graduate seminar on Beckett whose members, faced with the trilogy, sat in stunned silence. No one knew what to say or what these strange stories signified, although one or two spoke about Wittgenstein and Heidegger. It seemed to me, however, that allusions in the opening pages pointed to Dante and the Bible, although I did not have the courage then to say so.

From that moment to this, many persons have helped me. I am deeply indebted to the novelist Paul West, who guided the early drafts and who encouraged me to pursue my own vision of the significance of Beckett's allusions. Particular thanks go to the poet Josephine Jacobsen, who read the manuscript in its earliest stages and made constructive suggestions. I would also like to acknowledge the kind assistance of Mrs. Josephine M. Dearborn of the Bishop Payne Library, Virginia Theological Seminary, in researching the 1906 Anglican Hymnal.

I wish to thank most sincerely Peter Ross Sieger, whose editing skills are augmented by a fine understanding of the mainstream Christian denominations and whose patience in answering my questions was exemplary. I am grateful also to Sharon Ritchie, who uncomplainingly and speedily retyped many pages of the manuscript.

My warmest gratitude is owed to Giles Gunn and to Robert Boyle, S. J. During difficult times, their encouragement and constructive criticism, respectively, sustained me. I would also like to thank Grove Press, Inc., for permitting me to quote freely from the works of Samuel Beckett.

Preface

Above all, my grateful thanks are due to Mr. Samuel Beckett for his prompt and courteous replies to certain questions I asked him. "I was helped. I'd never have got there alone."

I

Celebration of Nothingness

> *Maximal negation is minimal affirmation.*
>
> Samuel Beckett

Reading Samuel Beckett's trilogy *(Molloy, Malone Dies, The Un-namable)* is an exhausting, irritating experience which produces either enervation and apathy or a sick exhilaration, like standing on a high and perilous ledge and contemplating what is below—or above. It is easy enough to lose one's sense of balance in this seemingly insane jumble of squalid characters, names all beginning with "M," who against a background of either "the city" or "the forest" perform incredible feats of endurance and legerdemain, without legs riding bicycles, crawling through the woods, living in jars, turning into each other. The author himself, using words like a master juggler, eventually jumps through hoops, balls and all. A good metaphor, that, considering that he is interested in nothing less than the most fabulous circle of all, call it God or zero. And jumping through hoops is a neat trick if you happen to be armless, legless, mute, blind, or suffering from prolapsed genitalia, in the manner of Beckett's characters.

When I first began to study the work of Samuel Beckett, in the 1960's, critics of his plays and novels appeared awed but somewhat baffled. However, the general impression at that time seemed to be, following Martin Esslin's lead, that Beckett is part of the theatre of the absurd and that his work portrays the impossibility of attaining meaning in an absurd world. The witnesses are numerous. Eric Bentley, in his essay "The Talent of Samuel Beckett" *(Casebook on Waiting for Godot,* Ruby Cohn, ed.), asserts that Beckett's view is close to that of Sartre, and says *Waiting for Godot* is the quintessence of existentialism. Raymond Federman, in *Journey to Chaos: Samuel Beckett's Early Fiction,* says: "As portrayed by Beckett's characters, man appears alienated from the source of his existence, cut off from reality and sur- rounded by the illusions he substitutes for the resulting void" (194).[1] According to John Fletcher (in *Samuel Beckett's Art*), "His fiction progresses towards a more and more total emptiness, in which plot, characters and language itself crumble to nothing, leaving only a voice awaiting the silence in fear and trembling" (144). In Lawrence Harvey's *Samuel Beckett: Poet and Critic* we find this comment: "The range of his response extends from sardonic irony to irreverent puns to a sorrowfully resigned state- ment of disillusionment. For him neither institutional change nor religious faith provides an effective antidote for the malady of existence" (124). Ihab Hassan in *Literature of Silence: Henry Miller and Samuel Beckett* detects "an ironic and perhaps a nihilis- tic view of the world and a sense of experience that is entirely private" (19).

All this is true enough; that is to say, half-true. Beckett re- ceived the 1969 Nobel Prize in Literature for singing the *dies irae* of the human race. But is that all there is? Were Beckett an author who courts and manipulates publicity, one might sus- pect that his work is all empty show—a mad pyrotechnic dis- play of virtuosity, seasoned with a *frisson* of revolting sadism. But he rarely gives interviews and although graciously accessi- ble to serious students, he maintains an inviolable privacy against the press. The work, therefore, stands virtually on its own, without benefit of a personality cult, movie contracts, orgies, divorces, or philosophical disquisitions in a pipe- scented, book-lined study. It must offer more than a sneer of disgust, or it could never have deployed its extraordinary *mana.*

Close reading of the Beckettian oeuvre reveals a structure as complex as, though different from, the structures of Dante, Langland, or T.S. Eliot, and carefully chosen diction with a cadence that speeds up and slows down, modulating into either scabrous humour or an awe-inspiring and mysterious lyri-

---

[1]The number in parentheses represents page numbers of volumes mentioned.

cism—a lyricism seldom discussed, by the way, by critics looking for nihilism amid the irony. In the end, Beckett's prose affects one like a cry in the twilight, to which attention must be paid. And underneath it all, like the shadowy walls of a buried town seen from the air, or like drowned cities wavering under water, are the lineaments of something else, another system, a point of view, a possibility, wildly at variance with Beckett's supposed opinions and attitudes.

A few of his early critics have glimpsed the possibility. In the midst of his explanation of Beckett's work as a study of schizophrenia (*Samuel Beckett: A New Approach. A Study of the Novels and Plays*), G. C. Barnard states: "Beckett is a mystic, but of an unusual type. . . . In Beckett's visions we find the ground of our Being is a terrible abyss from which the self recoils lest it should fall into annihilation" (19). But in Barnard's view, Beckett's "mystical" search is for the Self, and Barnard is more interested in psychiatric and psychoanalytic analyses than in considering the clue he himself has unravelled. Raymond Federman, too, notes that "the nothingness Murphy is here enjoying is that classical, mystical experience that all Beckett's French heroes seek in the depth of their own delirious unconsciousness" (71). Federman, however, takes a highly pejorative view of mysticism. To him Murphy is deliberately attempting to reach a state of mental alienation, or, in other words, insanity: "The selfless Beckett hero is driven on and on into an infinite inner world to be confronted in the end with his own void" (200). Although Lawrence Harvey notes that "Behind such lines [*Echo's Bones*] work a mind and heart filled with a deep sense of the unreality of the human wrapping and a strong faith in the presence—veiled, elusive, abortive even—of a being somehow independent, at least in part, of its surface covering" (71), he too takes an uncomprising anti-metaphysical line in discussing the poems. I believe that Beckett's poems looked at another way might yield quite other insights. Yet in spite of his own skepticism, Harvey is forced to remark of a poem to the Alba that it "attempts to put into words the experience of release into a kind of absence that is at the same time a mysterious presence, the experience of an extratemporal reality" (262). And he admits that "While the use of religious material for the purpose of art no doubt of itself implies neither belief nor disbelief, it does seem to indicate concern with a religious dimension" (277).

One critical team early on gave close attention to Beckett's preoccupation with Christian themes—Josephine Jacobsen and William Mueller in *The Testament of Samuel Beckett.* Yet although they see Beckett as "squarely . . . in the tradition of the Old Testament prophets and that of Paul, Augustine, and Calvin" (104), they sometimes seem to regard him as a singularly pure agnostic, one whose epistemology really does hang on that crucial "perhaps," and sometimes as a savagely disappointed mystic manqué who pursues the void because God has failed.

The majority of these earlier critics tended to ignore the religious language and the strong hints of mysticism in some of the works. With the passage of time, however, and with a gradual uncovering of all the recondite allusions, a more sophisticated view has emerged in the 1970's, heralded by Hugh Kenner's *Samuel Beckett: A Critical Study* in 1968. Written in a brilliant style—a work of art in itself—Kenner's analysis depends heavily on Descartes as the chief reference point in Beckettian thought. But, as Sighle Kennedy says in her book on *Murphy:* "If . . . Descartes represents a central line in Beckett's thought, my central argument in this study cannot hold" (55). On the other hand, Kenner does note the stripped-down condition of the characters in *Waiting for Godot* and explicitly compares it to St. John of the Cross's "famous minimal prescription" (152). He also mentions the fact that characters in other works listen to a "mysterious authority" (89). Both of these insights confirm my own sense that there are more things in Beckett's work than are dreamt of in philosophy.

Melvin Friedman's collection *Samuel Beckett Now* demonstrates the slight tilt in Beckett criticism toward the theological dimension. Friedman took the unprecedented step of mentioning G. S. Fraser's article in the *Times Literary Supplement* which read *Waiting for Godot* as "a modern morality play, on permanent Christian themes" and which mentions *Godot* in the same breath as *Everyman* and *Pilgrim's Progress* (21). Friedman also summarized comments by other Christian or Christian-oriented critics—those by Charles McCoy in *The Florida Review* (Spring, 1958), Ward Hooker in *The Kenyon Review* (Summer, 1960), and Heintz Politzer in *The Christian Scholar* (March,

1959), all of whom see *Waiting for Godot* as a religious parable or allegory and specifically a Christian one. In the same collection by Friedman, Frederick Hoffman claims that "Beckett's primary text [is] the creature straining to see and to define his creator" (45). Germaine Brée in the same volume sees the settings of Beckett's works as "related to medieval metaphysics: the universe of concentric zones, the symbolism of the circle and the center" (77). She also comments that Beckettian setting "is, on the whole, more in the tradition of Dante or of Milton; we sense a familiar metaphysical vision behind the imaginary structure" (78). And she sums up by saying that Beckett's monologue "does not progress . . . its only method, if it can be called a method, is in the mystic tradition; it illustrates the via negativa . . . " (122).

Three spendidly ample discussions of Beckett's work, David Hesla's *The Shape of Chaos*, Colin Duckworth's *Angels of Darkness*, and John Pilling's *Samuel Beckett*, all published in the seventies, vary in their assessment of how "religious" the works are, but all three take some serious and sophisticated account of the religious language and allusions in a manner which had not been customary earlier. Of course, other works continue to be published which reject any religious interest on the part of Beckett, for example, the two books by Eugene Webb, one on the plays, the other on the novels.

Climaxing this re-evaluation of Beckett came Deirdre Bair's biography in 1978. Her book offers no speculation as to the metaphysics of either Beckett himself or of his works, but does quote Beckett as denying that he consciously intended Godot to represent God in the play *Waiting for Godot* (557).

My own conviction that attention must be paid to the religious language and to the mysticism which seems to be inherent in much of the work began in the sixties, but my ideas were not summarized and delivered in a paper until 1978. Some of the insights offered by the Beckett critics of the seventies parallel mine, but since none takes exactly the same track, I have felt it reasonable to present these conclusions as they were originally written.

Beckett's work is certainly, among other things, an exploration of the available voices of fiction (the characters in the tale, the narrator, the literary author, the *real* author). In a way the three novels particularly are a series of variations which illustrate the range of technical possibilities of fiction. For Beckett as for most authors, writing is a compulsion, a word-game he has to play, and part of his anguish comes from the fact that he has hidden behind, lived through, his characters, rather than in his own self. Thus the trilogy and the plays demonstrate a shifting coalescence of masks and also a progressive stripping-off of them until the writer is down to the bare, forked "I" of *The Unnamable* or *Not I*. In fact, some see this search for the "I" as the meaning of the work, and to some extent it is. But what is beyond "I"? Who is writing this novel in which we are all characters? What is the end of our story? Is our world as "unreal" as the world created in fiction and drama? Or, if the novels and plays are "realer" than real, is the story composed by our creator—supposing we have one—realer than real? Thoughts such as these swirl in the head after reading *Waiting for Godot, The Lost Ones,* or the trilogy; one feels that however much Beckett may seem to mock metaphysics, it is really the only subject which interests him, and that not in a rational chop-logic way, but in a way intuitive, metaphorical, and mythic. In his own words to Tom Driver in the famous interview "Beckett by the Madeleine" (*Columbia University Forum,* Summer 1961): "When Heidegger and Sartre speak of a contrast between being and existence, they may be right, I don't know, but their language is too philosophical for me. I am not a philosopher" (22).

I would hazard the guess that the progressive stripping-down of the self which takes place in so many of Beckett's works is not just a search for self, but in fact the "negative way" of mysticism, whose object is to break the bonds of time and place and find what Eliot calls the still center of the turning world.

Beckett himself has said that if he were a critic setting out to write on the works of Beckett (and he thanked heaven he was not), he would start with two quotations, one by Geulincx[2] ("Ubi nihil valis ibi nihil velis"—"Where one values nothing one should will nothing"), and one by Democritus ("Nothing is more real than nothing") (Harvey, 267). One should neither neglect these comments nor trust them wholly. Beckett's friend

---

[2]Arnold Geulincx: Belgian philosopher, 1624–1669.

A. J. Leventhal, who has known him for a long time, has warned us in the special Beckett issue of *New Theatre Magazine:* ". . . it is a kind of humour on his part to divert you a little bit, to put you on the wrong scent" (14). Deirdre Bair also states in her biography of Beckett that he likes to create confusion about his work: "The more stories there are, the better I like it" (381). No truly great writer is voluntarily going to give away the figure in his carpet (supposing he can see it himself), and Beckett's explanations of his own work are not disingenuous. The only test of such remarks is to lay them within the magnetic field of a particular work and see if, so to speak, they light up. The comment on Geulincx is perhaps the more significant of the two, given that Beckett frequently refers to Geulincx and seldom to Democritus. Both the above remarks can be seen as expressing an essential detachment from the things of this world. And, as will be seen, the works I have chosen to discuss represent metaphorically a continuing process of stripping away, of detachment, as a preliminary to the mystic encounter.

Although I will present many other justifications for these assertions—such as plot, setting, and pilgrim character and the analogies of plot, setting, and pilgrim character to the works of Dante, Langland, and Eliot; the extreme use of extreme paradox; allusions to the Bible, Book of Common Prayer, and Hymnal—the main justification is Beckett's tone. This tone is not always and invariably one of cynical irony, but is fairly often one of dreamy wonder or lyrical yearning. Even the irony is not consistent in tone; it is much more savage where its object is sexuality or the functions of the body than when its object is man's metaphysical quest. Beckett's tone is by no means as uniformly destructive and nihilistic as has been supposed.

Any close explication of Beckett's work runs the risk of appearing to be as absurd a rational enterprise as the sucking-stone routine of Molloy. Let no skeptical reader assume that I attempt such explication without a considerable degree of self-irony. What impels me is the hope of revealing some of the layers of richness in these undramatic dramas and unnovelistic novels. Beckett's work is a synthesis of poetry, religion, philosophy, myth, etymology, erudition, and acute self-consciousness, arranged in formal structures, somewhat perhaps as Herman Hesse conceived the glass-bead game. As Bert O. States puts it in his brilliant *The Shape of Paradox: An Essay on Waiting for Godot,* Beckett "converts theology into poetry" (44). The rightness or wrongness of my glosses is unimportant; what is important is that, in spite of the differences of style, the works offer the same kind of literary richness we are accustomed to finding in Eliot and Dante.

Too many critics, obsessed with particular points of view, are pedantic or literal in their approach to Beckett, anxiously trying to turn him into a realistic novelist, or a clinical novelist, or a systematic Manichean. For example, Lawrence Harvey says in *Samuel Beckett: Poet and Critic* that Mr. Knott in *Watt* cannot "be" or represent God because many of his actions "surely never have been associated with the god of any known religion; his habits of dress and his gastronomic preferences, for example" (366). Such an approach seems excessively literal, particularly where one is dealing with a deeply ironic and symbolic writer like Beckett. Again, G. C. Barnard in *Samuel Beckett: A New Approach* soberly proves that all Beckett's work is a study of various forms of schizophrenia, in which Beckett is supposed to have become interested because of his relationship with Lucia, Joyce's mentally ill daughter.[3] For a third example, the Hamiltons, Kenneth and Alice, in *Condemned to Life: The World of Samuel Beckett,* assert that Beckett is a Manichean in a thorough-going and systematic sense, to the point where, according to the Hamiltons, he delivers anti-Christian polemics *because of* his Manicheanism.

Away with such reductionist approaches. For Beckett, there is one story and one story only that is worth telling, and that is the story of quest, of man in search of the ground of his being. In the short stories and in *Murphy,* the quest is represented in more or less realistic ways, in approximately "real" cities and situations. In the trilogy, however, and in *Waiting for Godot, Watt, The Lost Ones,* and *Not I,* the quest takes place in mythic landscapes and among symbolic characters that resemble the

---

[3]Barnard and others who take a psychological approach confuse the schizophrenic state with the mystical state. They are certainly similar in their outward manifestations, but one, the mystical, is wholesome and sustaining; the other is not. Joseph Campbell has explained the difference lucidly in his *Myths to Live By,* p. 209. Another helpful discussion of the difference between madness and mysticism is found in R.C. Zaehner's *Mysticism, Sacred and Profane,* Chapters V and VI.

dream landscapes and characters of *Piers the Ploughman* and *The Divine Comedy* more than they do those of *Ulysses* or Sartre's *The Flies* or *No Exit*.

A weakness which has affected criticism of Beckett is the awe which prevents recognition of a natural progression, growth, and change in Beckett's art, as in that of most writers. Few artists emerge full-blown and maintain the same high level of accomplishment during their entire artistic life. The result of this over-reverent attitude on the part of critics is that *Whoroscope* and *More Pricks Than Kicks* are taken on exactly the same level as Beckett's masterpieces, *Waiting for Godot* and the trilogy. Like Dante, Shakespeare, or Joyce, Beckett too was once young and brash; he had no magical exemption from shallowness, self-indulgence, or from just plain silliness. Fletcher, Harvey, and Kenner are outstanding in their perception of Beckett's immaturities, as they are outstanding Beckett critics in other respects. The important issue here is not which of Beckett's works are great or mature and which lesser or immature, but the fact that like anyone, Beckett may have grown out of certain preoccupations and immaturities of style, may have changed his views and his style from time to time, perhaps may have returned to earlier values or asserted new ones, with consequent change in style.

In assessing the Beckett oeuvre to date, I see a line of development which can be expressed schematically as follows: First, the early period (1929–1945), in which Beckett is much under the influence of Joyce and Eliot. The work of this period (*Whoroscope, More Pricks Than Kicks, Echo's Bones, Murphy,*), is full of ultra-clever word-play and satiric jibes, often at religion or at religious figures and symbols. In the middle period (1946–1956), the sobering effects of the war and the Resistance movement are evident. In spite of the pervasive irony, *Watt, Godot,* and the trilogy are basically mystical and concerned with theological concepts, and are full of religious allusions. The later middle period (1956–1966) displays increasing despair and nausea as the influence of the war wears off (*All That Fall, How It Is, Krapp's Last Tape, Embers, Endgame, Happy Days*). From 1966 to the present, there appears to be a turning back to the mood of the early middle period (*The Lost Ones, Not I*).

In this study I do not intend to discuss period one or period three. The works of these periods have been treated exhaustively and brilliantly by others. Furthermore, at this reading, only the works of periods two and four can be subsumed under the rubric of mysticism and metaphysical quest I am attempting to outline here.

The influence of St. Augustine, Descartes, and Dante upon Beckett has already been established by many critics and scholars, while the influence of T. S. Eliot upon Beckett has only been noted by Lawrence Harvey. The latter influence is not unlikely, since both Eliot and Beckett were good friends of Joyce, and Eliot's reputation as poet and critic was extremely high at the time that both he and Beckett were intimates of the Joyce family (see *Letters of James Joyce,* ed. Richard Ellmann, Vol. 3, *passim*). But further study demonstrates that at least part of the similarity between Eliot and Beckett occurs because they both draw on common sources: Heraclitus, St. Augustine, Dante, Pascal, Herbert, the mystical tradition in Christianity generally. The fact that one became a vestryman in the Church of England and that the other appears to stand outside Christianity is irrelevant to the common sources of the works.

My use of parallels drawn from Simone Weil's work may be questioned, particularly the use of *Waiting for God,* which was published first in France in 1950, while *Waiting for Godot* and the trilogy were written in 1947–1949, although not published till 1951–1953. Certain facts are highly suggestive of some possible connection between Weil and Beckett. First of all, Simone Weil was a student at the École Normale Superieure at the same time Beckett was teaching there (1928–1930). Since she was known to be a strikingly intelligent and outstanding student, it is difficult to believe he did not hear of her. Secondly, they both worked in the Resistance and in the vineyards of the south of France; although their paths may never have crossed geographically and indeed appear not to have, it is not impossible that they knew of each other as Resistance patriots. They both fled south from Paris in June, 1940, but while Simone Weil went to Marseilles and worked in the vineyards in the summer of 1941, Beckett returned to Paris as an agent of the Resistance until the Gestapo closed in and he fled south again, to the Vaucluse, where he worked in the vineyards in 1942. In 1942 Weil was making her abortive journey to the United

States and thence to England where she died. In reply to my inquiry, Mr. Beckett stated that he did not know Simone Weil and was "little acquainted with her works." The latter phrase of course could mean anything or nothing at all. It seems likely that at least the title, and possibly the content, of *Waiting for Godot* is an allusion to Simone Weil's *Waiting for God.*[4]

We must remember Bair's comment that Beckett likes to create confusion about his work; the need to deny the figure in his carpet may cause him to play down his knowledge of Simone Weil. In any case, Simone Weil is acknowledged to be a Christian mystic although she refused to be baptized. Since she is a mystic and a contemporary of Beckett's, it seems fair enough to use passages from her works along with those of some other mystics of more venerable tradition, to show similarities of thought and expression to those of Beckett.

Given the climate of modern thought, it is perhaps necessary to state once and for all that to associate Beckett with Christian writers and metaphysical quests does not necessarily entail the kind of belief in God or Christian dogma long held by institutional Christians. The majority of Beckett's critics appear to see only these alternatives: that one is either a professing member of an institutional church *or* a nonbeliever in any metaphysical entity. This point of view is common in our secular world but probably inaccurate. Even for professing Christians, "belief" is seldom as hard and fast an affair as atheists and agnostics conceive it to be.

Apart from what the plays and novels may hint, the crucially important statement of Beckett's "religious" position is, to my mind, in the interview with Tom Driver. In Beckett's few other public statements about his work, he is talking to those whom he wittily—and contemptuously—calls the "chartered recountants" or those who commit "hysterectomies with a trowel"— literary men or academics little concerned with metaphysical speculation or actively hostile to it. But Beckett surely knew that in talking with Tom Driver he was not only communicating with a literary critic but with a theologian. Thus his enig-

---

[4]A little-noted article by Robert S. Cohen, "Parallels and the Possibility of Influence Between Simone Weil's *Waiting for God* and Samuel Beckett's *Waiting for Godot*," discusses the similarities of content.

matic remarks to Driver have a peculiar significance and de-
serve to be considered very seriously:

> If life and death did not both present themselves to us,
> there would be no inscrutability. If there were only dark-
> ness, all would be clear. *It is because there is not only darkness
> but also light that our situation becomes inexplicable.* Take Au-
> gustine's doctrine of grace given and grace withheld: have
> you pondered the dramatic qualities in this theology? Two
> thieves are crucified with Christ, one saved and the other
> damned. How can we make sense of this division? . . .
> where we have both dark and light we have the inexplica-
> ble. The key word in my plays is "perhaps." (24, italics
> mine)

The last sentence is often loosely quoted; the attentive reader
will note that Beckett does not use "perhaps" here to refer to
the existence of God, but to refer to damnation and salvation.

It is true that in the same interview, Beckett said, "I have no
religious feeling. Once I had a religious emotion. It was my
first communion. No more." In the same dialogue he described
his mother's devout Protestantism as useless at the time of her
death, but pronounced Irish Catholicism as "deeper." For himself, his native Protestantism was "only irksome," and he let it
go.

Yet William Mueller, Josephine Jacobsen, and John Fletcher
in the sixties, and David Hesla, Colin Duckworth, and John
Pilling in the seventies, have noted his almost obsessive preoccupation with Christianity and Christian themes. Almost every
one of his works considers the problems of evil and of unmer-
ited suffering, the question of free will, the possibility of redemption and salvation. These topics are not only considered,
but considered specifically in the Christian context and in symbolism and terms of reference which are Christian, *malgré* those
critics who wish to dub Beckett a Zen Buddhist. The materialist
and secularist ethos of our time and Beckett's own perhaps
misleading statements about his religious position have all con-
spired to prevent recognition that *Watt, Waiting for Godot,* the
trilogy, *The Lost Ones,* and *Not I* are ideograms or metaphorical
diagrams of theological concepts, particularly mystical ones.
Harvey, for example, says of the "deity" in Godot: "The three

terms [absence of suffering, of brilliance, and of speech] describe accurately enough the indifferent, darkly mysterious, and uncommunicative Almighty of Beckett's vision" (367), which somehow suggests that this view of God is peculiarly Beckett's own and into the bargain is faintly unorthodox or heretical. Certainly, this view of God is different from the popular one; but then, almost by definition, all popular views are debased forms of the real thing. One has only to look at popular views of Freud or Marx to realize the discrepancy. The "indifferent, darkly mysterious, and uncommunicative Almighty" is not only the God of Beckett's vision. He is the God of Job's, of Isaiah's, even of Christ's vision—at certain times.

It might be said here that all the way through his brilliant study, Harvey notes the hints of mystical experience in Beckett's early poems and fiction, but does not do very much with them. Others have noted Beckett's acute self-consciousness. The two indications are not necessarily contradictory. Persons who are acutely conscious of self are precisely the kind of persons who might wish to lose the self in the divine, the all, the Atman, or whatever one wishes to call it. As T. S. Eliot said so finely about the losing of the self in art ("Tradition and the Individual Talent," *Selected Essays*), "only those who have personality and emotions know what it means to want to escape from these things" (10).

Throughout the Beckettian canon the most sacred terms of reference in Christian theology are juxtaposed to the plainest, most downright, disgusted and disgusting references to basic functions of the body, which appear completely inappropriate to the mystical pursuit. Indeed, most critics see this juxtaposition as irony at the expense of religion. Perhaps it is, but Beckett's enormous preoccupation with religious matters suggests otherwise. Ample precedent for such startling juxtapositions exists in orthodox Christian thought and in the work of Eliot, Dante, and Langland. The body is, after all, a hindrance to the vision of God; it is, in its ambivalent desires, responsible for the estrangement from God, and is therefore viewed with loathing by those dedicated to the pursuit of the divine. This is not a fashionable point of view today, when Christians are determinedly seeing all Creation as good, happily celebrating, along with secular minds, the joys of the flesh as well as those of the spirit.

Even in the great high periods of mysticism—the Middle Ages and the seventeenth century—there have been two strains of thought as regards the body and its functions: affirmative and negative. The more affirmative mystics, such as St. Francis, have looked on the body with affection and tolerance; the negative ones have despised the body, and to this group Beckett belongs. In Beckett's case, however, the mystic's sense that the body is an interference and distraction in the search for the divine is overlaid with a Manichean horror of sexual activity.

The relationship of Beckett's style—above all, his tone—to what I assert is his subject matter will be discussed later. One thing should be said, however. Since the works I will discuss were, with one exception, first written in French and later translated into English, any interpretive theory based only on the English translation may appear highly suspect. Yet, on closer study, it will be seen that this objection does not apply. Beckett himself made the translations for all of the works discussed here except *Watt*, which was originally written in English, and *Molloy*, in which Beckett collaborated with Patrick Bowles. Presumably he chose allusions or English surrogates which, *in the same context as that read by French persons*, would have particular meaning for English readers. Doubtless, in the French versions, the allusions were chosen to have particular meaning for French readers. But the context, the "plot" elements, in all the works remains the same—the protagonists who gradually shed their possessions and their worldly preoccupations and who wander a purgatorial landscape searching for Mr. Knott, Mr. Godot, the "real silence," or their "lost ones." It cannot be supposed that the country of St. Bernard, St. Thérèse, St. Joan, and Simone Weil would not comprehend the mystical quest, while English readers would. The evidence adduced for my theory lies as much in the story lines as in the language used, but also of course does lie in the language used—in this case the English language. Obviously, this study would not be conceivable if Beckett had not made or supervised his own translations. Although I am of French descent and am reasonably bilingual, limitations of time and human ability prevent me from applying the same theory twice, once to the English and once to the French versions. This must be done by others if it is done at all. But I am convinced that the theory that these works of Beckett's represent metaphorically the mystic quest will hold for the French versions as well as the English ones.

My view is, I hope, neither reductive nor exclusive, yet it does take certain assumptions about Beckett's work for granted, as already demonstrated. That I think certain novels and plays may be seen as a cumulative metaphor for the successive stages of the mystic quest must not be taken to imply that this is *all* they are. I have no wish to ignore the comic inventiveness, the satire of man's institutions and frailties, the despairing view of man's capacity to transcend his divided nature, the gloating travesty of infirmity and old age, the surrealism and absurdity of these self-destructing novels and plays, all of which have already been established by others as components of Beckett's style and values. But here these components are seen in relation to a context whose origins go back to Dante and St. Augustine.

II

The Still Center:
Mysticism and Mystic Discipline

A God comprehended is no God

Teerstegen

To say what mysticism is without being misunderstood is extremely difficult. In his famous *Studies of English Mystics,* Dean Inge offered twenty-six definitions of mysticism. Instead of rehearsing these, let us rather say what it is not. It is not spiritualism or occultism, such as Yeats was interested in. Nor is it vague religious emotionalism or nebulous idealism. The phrase "all religion is mystical," sometimes heard among those interested in the subject, should be rephrased to read "all religion can be, or perhaps should be, mystical." But that religion is not necessarily mystical is perfectly evident. Religion does postulate the "something beyond," or "other," which so preoccupies the mystic, but in practice, all religions infrequently lead to direct contact with the "other."

As used in this paper and in relation to Beckett and his work, I shall define mysticism as direct experience of or contact with Absolute or Unconditioned Being, or with what is called in orthodoxy—God.

Mysticism may be expressed in the words of St. Augustine, with whose writings we know Beckett to be very familiar: "And thus with the flash of one trembling glance it [my mind] arrives at That Which Is" (*Confessions,* Book VIII.)[5] While Augustine

[5]Many of the writings of the mystics are not yet available in English and some are not easily available at all. For the convenience of the

and earlier Christian mystics lay stress upon contemplation and the unitive state, the later mystics, such as St. John of the Cross, influenced by the Pseudo-Dionysius, emphasized darkness and obscurity. According to Dom Cuthbert Butler, in his book *Western Mysticism,* they speak "of knowing God by ignorance and unknowing; of being plunged in the solitude of the Godhead or in the viewless abyss of the Divine Nature" (123). For example:

> The mystics heap up terms of negation—darkness, void, nothingness—in endeavoring to describe that Absolute which they have apprehended. It may be, of course, that their apprehension had such a fullness and richness of content that in human language it could only be described negatively. (123)

Butler quotes a professor of psychology who describes the negative way as "the effacement of the empiric self, the abandonment of imagery and spatiality, the absence of all multiplicity—that is, in a word, the cessation of conceptual thought" (1). The similarity of this to what Beckett appears to be describing, particularly in the trilogy, is striking. The state may be further illustrated by extracts from the works of two actual mystics, the first from the Pseudo-Dionysius, the second from the anonymous author of the English fourteenth-century treatise *The Cloud of Unknowing:*

> [The mind] enters into the really mystic Darkness of Unknowing wherein it renounces all the perceptions of the understanding, and abides in That Which is wholly intangible and invisible, belonging wholly to Him that is beyond all, through being by inactivity of all cognition united in its highest part to Him Who is wholly unknowable, and by

---

reader, the sources used for the writings of St. Augustine and the other mystics quoted throughout are, unless otherwise noted, F. C. Happold, *Mysticism: A Study and an Anthology,* Elmer O'Brien, *Varieties of Mystic Experience,* and Rudolph Otto, *The Idea of the Holy.* These collections were recommended by Fr. Georges Tavard, a distinguished Roman Catholic scholar, ecumenist, and theologian, in his course on mysticism given at the Pennsylvania State University in 1968. I have not used Evelyn Underhill's *Mysticism* because it may be regarded as popularized treatment and insufficiently scholarly.

knowing nothing knows in a manner that is above all understanding.

> Then will He sometimes peradventure send out a beam of ghostly lights, piercing this cloud of unknowing that is betwixt thee and Him; and shew thee some of His privity, the which man may not, nor cannot speak. (Butler, 6)

Books on mysticism suggest many different categories and variants of mysticism, depending on the metaphysical or religious predilections of the writers. One of the most useful is that of F. C. Happold in his study-anthology called *Mysticism*. Happold divides mysticism into three kinds: nature-mysticism, soul-mysticism, and God-mysticism. In nature-mysticism (what Auden calls rather archly "The vision of Dame Kind"), the soul experiences communion with the divine in or through nature and all created things. Most of what seem to be mystical experiences in *Molloy* are of this type. In soul-mysticism, the soul, stripped of every possession and preoccupation, contacts its own absoluteness, its Self. This type of mysticism is common among Eastern adepts. God-mysticism often overlaps either of the two, and all three forms may be seen as successive stages.

In the mystical experience, the soul returns to the ground of its being in a communion which, though transient, takes place outside of time and space. The grace of union with the divine is random and unpredictable; frequency can, however, be increased by practice and discipline.

The state of union with the divine and indeed what we might call the metaphysic of mysticism are indescribable except by means of metaphor or by paradoxical negatives. For example, the Pseudo-Dionysius says: "By knowing nothing he [the mystic] knows that Which is beyond his knowledge" (Happold, 193). Another remarkable passage from the Pseudo-Dionysius illustrates perfectly the paradoxical method:

> Into this Dark beyond all light, we pray
> to come and,
> unseeing and unknowing,
> to see and
> to know
> Him that is

beyond seeing and
beyond knowing
precisely by not seeing,
by not knowing.
For that is truly to see and
to know and
to hymn transcendently
Him that transcends all.
That is, negating, to do as sculptors do,
drawing [from marble]
the statue latent there,
removing all that
hinders or
hides
the pure spectacle of the hidden form and
displaying, with this mere removal,
the beauty hidden there.
One must, I think, hymn in
negating and
affirming
for affirmations proceed
from the topmost
through the middlemost
to the lowest.
But here,
from the lowest
to the topmost,
One denies them all, thus
to lay bare the Unknowable who is
by all known beings veiled,
to see the transcendent Dark that is
by the light of being hid.

(O'Brien, 72–73)

Saint Gregory expressed the paradox more succinctly: "But if one asks for an interpretation or description or explanation of the divine nature we shall not deny that in such a science as this we are unlearned. . . . For there is no way of comprehending the indefinable as it is by a scheme of words. For the Divine is too noble and too lofty *to be indicated by a name;* and we have learned to honour by silence that which transcends reason and thought" (Otto, 185–186, italics mine).

Similarly, in his book *Of Learned Ignorance,* a title which is in itself a paradox, Nicholas of Cusa says: "The place wherein Thou [Absolute Being] are found unveiled is girt round with the coincidence of contradictories" (Happold, 305), a marvellous phrase which would serve extremely well as a description of Beckett's writing. Much of his work is full of paradoxes or contraries. Here are several examples taken at random:

> . . . of being so light and free that it is as the being of nothing. (*Watt,* 40)

> Perhaps there is no whole before you're dead. (*Molloy,* 35)

> . . . there could be no things but nameless things, no names but thingless names. (*Molloy,* 41)

> Standing before my high window I gave myself to them [lights], waiting for them to end, for my joy to end, straining towards the joy of ended joy. (*Malone Dies,* 31)

> I shall have to speak of things of which I cannot speak. (*The Unnamable,* 4)

Many, many more could be found; especially in *The Unnamable* the text often consists of one paradox after another. Of course, paradox is not a tool exclusive to Beckett or the mystics, However, the extreme use of it by both suggests some connection independent of other evidence.

The mystic experience is not attainable at will; quite the reverse, the will and the ego must be relinquished, so that the soul can be grasped by the Absolute. "The mystic feels as if his own will were in abeyance, as if he were grasped and held by a power not his own," says F. C. Happold in the introduction to his anthology of mystical writers (46). This passivity is the "waiting on God" experience described by Simone Weil, among others: "In our acts of obedience to God we are passive . . . there is only waiting, attention, silence, immobility . . . " (147). Unfortunately, ambiguity has always plagued the history of mysticism; it is often difficult to tell whether the seeming inaction is silent waiting upon God or despairing and self-centered *akedia* (the central sin in the *Purgatorio* and in Eliot's *The Waste*

Land.) This confusion may be at least partly responsible for the prevalent view of Beckett as a nihilist.

The soul prepares itself for the experience by using the so-called mystic disciplines, which are not in themselves mystic at all. The first and most important requirement is for the soul to purge itself of all egotistical concerns. According to Happold, "The way of purgation has two main objectives: first of all, complete detachment from and renunciation of the things of the sense, and the death of the egocentric life,[6] so that the divine life may be born in the soul and union with the Godhead attained; and secondly, a continuous cleansing of the perceptions and a scouring of the windows of the soul, so that the light of a new reality may stream in and completely illuminate and transform it" (58). Or, as the anonymous author of the *Theologia Germanica* puts it:

> For the essential existence of God is without this and that, and without selfhood and I-hood, and the like; but it is the nature and property of the creature to seek itself and its own things, and this and that, here and there, and in all that it does and leaves undone its desire is to its own advantage and benefit. Now where a creature or a man denies and forsakes himself and his own and his selfhood, there God enters in with His own, that is, with Himself. (O'Brien, 162)

As will be seen, Beckett's Moran begins a course of detachment; he starts with a small family in relative affluence and loses all to wander the world as what we must call a pilgrim, although Beckett does not call him that. Molloy begins alone with few possessions and gradually loses even them. Malone is moribund in bed with only the most minimal personal apparatus, most of which is gone by the time he has his vision of the lights. And the narrator of *The Unnamable* appears to be speaking from a void. Watt is a wandering tramp with no possessions to speak of, as are Estragon and Vladimir in *Waiting for Godot*. In *The Lost Ones,* possessions, things, are simply not mentioned;

[6]Cf. T. S. Eliot: "Attachment to self and to things and persons, detachment/ From self and from things and from persons; and growing between them indifference/ Which resembles the others as death resembles life . . ." (*Four Quartets, Little Gidding,* III).

they have no validity in comparison with the all-important search for the lost ones. The female protagonist of *Not I* appears to be poor, or at any rate, not wealthy.

To those accustomed to thinking of mysticism in terms of the Christian saints, it may be absurd or even shocking to think of Beckett's moribunds in connection with mysticism. In the Christian tradition, of course, ethical purity of soul and love of God and fellowman are basic requirements of the mystic. However, it must be emphasized that the spiritual visitation may come to one whose soul is far from morally perfect. Mysticism in and of itself is amoral. Obviously, however, the self-purgation required would tend to make a person at least temporarily nonviolent and non-lustful, even though he might not be charitable and actively loving. Nevertheless, his sense of unity with God and therefore with all created things is difficult to separate from loving concern for others, although the latter may not be overt or apparent. It is in this light that we must see the habitual, though not continuous, dreamy diffidence of Beckett's characters.

As a consequence of purgation, the soul enters "the Dark Night," a phrase made famous in connection with the poetry of St. John of the Cross and of T. S. Eliot. Actually, there are two dark nights, according to St. John: "the first night or purgation is of the sensual part of the soul; and the second is of the spiritual part" (Happold, 327). To make matters more confusing, mystics often describe the unitive experience *itself* in terms of darkness: " . . . the higher part of contemplation . . . hangeth all wholly in this darkness and in this cloud of unknowing; with a loving stirring and blind beholding of the naked being of God Himself only," says the anonymous author of *The Cloud of Unknowing* (Happold, 281). Nicholas of Cusa speaks of entering into the darkness: "It behoveth, then, the intellect to become ignorant and to abide in darkness if it would fain see Thee" (Happold, 308). Conventionally, however, the divine has always been symbolized by light; for example, the Shekinah or Light of Glory of Judaism, symbolized by the burning bush of Moses. The mystic Ruysbroeck, for instance, says, "And from out the divine unity, there shines unto him [the mystic] a simple light; and this light shows him Darkness and Nakedness and Nothingness" (Happold, 256). And St. John of the Cross writes: "That near to God and round about Him are darkness and cloud; not that this is so in fact, but that it is so to our weak understanding, which is blinded and darkened by so vast a light, to which it cannot attain" (O'Brien, 223). Thus one would expect any metaphorical description of the mystical experience paradoxically to speak of lights in the darkness, or, as Otto puts it in his remarkable book, *The Idea of the Holy:*

> The darkness must be such as is enhanced and made all the more perceptible by contrast with some last vestige of brightness, which it is, as it were, on the point of extinguishing; hence the "mystical" effect begins with semidarkness . . . . The semidarkness that glimmers in vaulted halls, or beneath the branches of a lofty forest glade, strangely quickened and stirred by the mysterious play of half-lights, has always spoken eloquently to the soul . . . . (68)

There are no "vaulted halls" in Beckett's works, but plenty of glimmers in forest glades. Otto points out that art must represent the *mysterium tremendum* indirectly, and that darkness and silence are two of the modes most commonly used: "Of directer methods our Western art has only two, and they are in a noteworthy way, negative, viz. darkness and silence" (68).

Turning to the trilogy, we find that both the Molloy and Moran sections of *Molloy* stress darkness, that Molloy's story ends with a vision of light, as does Malone's, and that in *The Unnamable* the darkness is illuminated by the sunset sky, which is likened to Christ's blood streaming in the firmament. Watt arrives at Mr. Knott's house, a paradigm of the Lord's house or the church, in darkness, and he leaves it in the night also, although the moon shines on both occasions. Vladimir notes, in *Waiting for Godot,* that "it [the coming of Godot] is always at nightfall"(46). The whole of *The Lost Ones* takes place in a "dim yellowish light" (7). *Not I* takes place in the dark with one light only highlighting the speaking mouth of the protagonist.

Second only to darkness, silence is the metaphor most often used by the mystic to indicate the presence of the divine. As Herman says in *The Meaning and Value of Mysticism:* "All the great master mystics . . . invariably found that the Eternal can only be experienced in a profound and brooding silence extending even to thought and desire" (28). The Pseudo-Dionysius speaks of "the dazzling dark of the welcoming silence" (O'Brien, 69).

Ruysbroeck says, "This is the dark silence in which all lovers are lost" (O'Brien, 158), and Meister Eckhart eloquently uses the same metaphor:

> There is a saying of the wise man: "When all things lay in the midst of silence then leapt there down into me from on high, from the royal throne, a secret word." . . . But, Sir, where is the silence and where the place in which the word is spoken? As I said just now, it is in the purest part of the soul, in the noblest, in her ground, aye in the very essence of the soul. (Happold, 245–246)

In a beautiful passage in *Waiting for God*, the modern mystic, Simone Weil, speaks of the "silence" she encountered while repeating the "Our Father" while working in the vineyards:

> At times the very first words tear my thoughts from my body and transport it to a place outside space where there is neither perspective nor point of view. The infinity of the ordinary expanses of perception is replaced by an infinity to the second or sometimes the third degree. At the same time, filling every part of this infinity of infinity, there is silence, a silence which is not an absence of sound but which is the object of a positive sensation, more positive than that of sound. Noises, if there are any, only reach me after crossing this silence. (72)

The relevance of the metaphor of silence to Beckett's trilogy is most striking, for in the last book the narrator is constantly trying to attain what he calls "the real silence," although he expresses his yearning in floods of well-chosen words.

Basic to all mysticism is the hiddenness of God, a religious concept of which modern secular thinkers seem unaware. Anyone who understands the basic concepts of theology is surprised by secular interpretations of *Watt* and *Waiting for Godot*, which assume that Mr. Knott's invisibility and Godot's failure to appear in person indicate their nonexistence. Regardless of what may be thought of it in the twentieth century, the hiddenness of God is a thoroughly orthodox doctrine attested to by such diverse writers as George Herbert and Simone Weil. Primarily a way of expressing His transcendence rather than His immanence, God's hiddenness is established very early in the

Old Testament. Probably the earliest reference is in Exodus 33:20: "And he said, Thou canst not see my face: for there shall no man see me, and live." In other parts of the Old Testament, God allows himself to be seen or appears directly to individuals, but with a certain divine reserve, or holding back of his glory. The relationship to God, however, is a two-way street; the people also hold back, through their selfishness and blindness. Then they see but do not perceive. God said to Moses: ". . . I will hide my face from them and they shall be devoured and many evils and troubles shall befall them . . . . And I will surely hide my face on that day for all the evils which they shall have wrought, in that they are turned unto other gods" (Deut. 31:17–18). Similarly Isaiah waits upon God: "And I will wait upon the Lord, that hideth his face from the house of Jacob, and I will look for him" (Isa. 8:17). In Psalms 10:11 the psalmist tells us: "God has forgotten, he has hidden his face. . . ." The hiddenness of God is also maintained in the New Testament. For example, in 1 Timothy 1:17, Paul says: "The King of Ages, immortal, invisible, the only God," and in 1 Timothy 6:15–16: ". . . the Blessed and only Sovereign, the King of Kings and Lord of Lords, who alone has immortality and dwells in unapproachable light, whom no man has ever seen or can see."[7]

It must be stressed, however, that while God's apparent immanence does not prove God's existence, God's hiddenness or seeming absence equally does not mean his nonexistence. According to tradition and revelation, He does reveal Himself, on occasion, and the various theophanies are signaled by the traditional imagery of light, wind, and fire (Exod. 19 and 20).

Nevertheless, the hiddenness and otherness of the divine lead to describing and defining God in terms of negations, as we have already seen. According to Otto, "Not content with contrasting it [the Wholly Other] with all that is of nature or this world, mysticism concludes by contrasting it with Being itself and all that 'is,' and finally actually calls it 'that which is nothing.' By this 'nothing' is meant not only that of which noth-

---

[7]See also Pascal, *Pensée* 335, which is too long to quote, and *Pensées* 591 and 598, all three of which emphasize the hiddenness of God, and the theological necessity of God's being partially hidden, partially revealed.

ing can be predicated, but that which is absolutely and intrinsically other than and opposite of everything that is and can be thought" (29). Thus the "nothing" or "void," as Otto also calls it, so far from being the despairing nihilism which secular critics see in these works of Beckett's, may be the very Ground of Being. To quote Otto, again, "For 'void' is like darkness and silence, a negation, but a negation that does away with every 'this' and 'here' in order that the 'wholly other' may become actual" (70).

The objection that Beckett does not mean his void and his nothingness in this paradoxically affirmative way can only be answered by precisely the kind of explication of the texts, and more particularly of their tone, which I undertake here. Indubitably Beckett's tone is often ironic, not to say mocking or joking, but many parts of the trilogy and other works have a different tone altogether—either one of anguished yearning or of simple, spontaneous serenity—with no trace of irony whatever.

That Beckett is quite familiar with the mystical literature is obvious from the allusions to mystic discipline in *The Unnamable* (44–45, 77) and from satiric references in the early works. For example, Harvey tells us that in *Dream of Fair to Middling Women,* which Beckett refuses to publish, he speaks of himself as a "dud mystic," and calls himself "John of the Crossroads . . . a borderman" (326–327), a punning allusion to St. John of the Cross. The *Dream* also contains a reference to the mystic Pseudo-Dionysius: "That was the circular movement of the mind flowering up and up through darkness to an apex, dear to Dionysius the Areopagite" (343). In the short story, "Assumption," (*Transition,* June, 1929), there is a description of the mystical state (Harvey, 299). In *More Pricks Than Kicks,* there is an allusion to the mystic Jacob Boehme and to the English medieval mystic, Juliana of Norwich, whose words "all manner of thing shall be well" were quoted by T. S. Eliot in Section V of *Little Gidding,* with which I assume Beckett to be familiar; and Pilling states that "Murphy's self-laceration is . . . strangely reminiscent, even down to details, of the career of the thirteenth-century mystic, Henry Suso" (121).

It has long been noted by Beckett scholars that he seems to have been influenced philosophically by St. Augustine, Descartes, and Geulincx. To these figures I would add Pascal, whose *Pensées* can serve as a perfect gloss on both *Waiting for Godot* and the trilogy. In her essay "Philosophical Fragments in the Works of Samuel Beckett" (*Samuel Beckett: A Collection of Critical Essays*, Martin Esslin, ed.), Ruby Cohn does not include Pascal as an influence. However, Harvey notes allusions to Pascal in two or three of the poems. It would require another whole book to prove the point, but to me the influence of Pascal appears as great as, if not greater than, that of Descartes and Geulincx.[8] Pascal, of course, took the Augustinian side in his dispute with the Jesuits, another link with Beckett, whose interest in St. Augustine is well known.

Critics who are themselves committed to a secular point of view and who regard Beckett as being of their persuasion, are in some difficulty in attempting to show exactly how Augustine or Geulincx has influenced Beckett. Descartes is easier to deal with because Descartes was openly committed to the operations of reason. It can, however, truly be said of all these men, rational and intelligent though they were, that they were quite convinced there are large areas of life where reason cannot go. For example, in *Pensée* 4, we find Pascal saying, "If we submit everything to reason, there will be no mystery and no supernatural element in our religion. If we violate the principles of reason, our religion will be absurd, and it will be laughed at." More will be said of Geulincx later, but it is noteworthy that Augustine, Descartes, and Pascal each had a mystical experience—Augustine at his conversion in the garden in Milan, Descartes in the *poêle* or "hot cupboard" as recounted in De Baillet's life of Descartes, which Beckett knows well, and Pascal during the night of November 23, 1654. Thus Beckett is in the odd position, for a supposed atheist, of having been influenced by three of the most intelligent men in the history of the world—two of them scientists, for whatever that is worth—who managed to reconcile reason and intuition, intellect and insight, the visible and the invisible.

[8]For the influence of Descartes and Geulincx on Beckett, see John Fletcher, *The Novels of Samuel Beckett*, Lawrence Harvey, *Samuel Beckett: Poet and Critic*, David Hesla, *The Shape of Chaos: An Interpretation of the Art of Samuel Beckett*, and John Pilling, *Samuel Beckett*.

III

The Strait Gate:
The Quest of Molloy and Moran

We strode across that lonely plain like men
Who seek the road they strayed from . . . . "

Dante

The story of Molloy is a religious allegory—the story of a quest or pilgrimage—in which the protagonist tries out a home (that of Sophia Lousse), leaves it, and eventually ends in a mystical trance in a ditch.

Molloy begins his quest reasonably well-equipped (7). He has crutches, a hat, a mother, a bicycle with various accessories, but by the end of his quest he has lost or cares nothing about these. The opening page of the novel is an evocation of the endless cycle of life in which the mother reaches senescence and dies, and then the son comes to the same point. Whether the mother should be considered a mother in the factual and literal sense is questionable. Molloy is writing his story ("not for money"); he seems unclear as to whether he too has a son or not. Someone comes always on Sunday and takes away the pages as he writes them. Molloy makes a great point of the fact that "Here's my beginning"; in fact, he repeats the phrase twice. But when we read the "beginning," it turns out to be perhaps the beginning of something (the quest?), but not of Molloy's life, which is nearing its end. The phrasing reminds one of T. S. Eliot's "In my end is my beginning," (originally the motto on Mary Stuart's ring). Another striking phrase is "the things that are left," which in the context of death and farewell reminds us of the

28

"last things" in the rites of the church. Thus, in spite of the seemingly cynical bravado of "piss and shit in her pot," the opening of the trilogy strikes an implacably serious note: man is confronting death and pondering the other "last things"— judgment, hell, and heaven. Corroboration for this interpretation can be found in the text: "Then you try to pay attention, to consider with attention all those dim things" (9). The word "attention" is constantly used by Christian saints and mystics, for example, St. Ignatius of Loyola and St. Teresa of Avila, to indicate the manner in which spiritual exercises should be carried out. Simone Weil comments on attention in her essay, "Reflection on the Right Use of School Studies" in *Waiting for God:* " . . . prayer consists of attention [105] . . . . Quite apart from explicit religious belief every time that a human being succeeds in making an effort of attention with the sole idea of increasing his grasp of truth, he acquires a greater aptitude for grasping it, even though his effort produces no visible fruit . . . . There is a real desire when there is an effort of attention . . . . Even if our efforts of attention seem for years to be producing no result one day a light which is in exact proportion to them will flood the soul" (107–8). Note the reference to the light flooding the soul, so common among mystics; light is a frequently used image in the trilogy. Simone Weil then makes a distinction between the effort of the will and the passive but alert openness which is her definition of attention. She goes on: "Attention consists of suspending our thought, leaving it detached, empty and ready to be penetrated by the object . . . " (111). Later we shall see how Beckett's questers gradually achieve this kind of "attention." Here it is sufficient to give one more quotation from Weil's chapter on attention, which links her thought not only to the trilogy, but also to *Waiting for Godot:* "We do not obtain the most precious gifts by going in search of them but *by waiting for them"* (112, italics mine). As we shall see, Molloy, Moran, and Malone do go in search, but eventually cease active searching in favor of passive but alert waiting, while the book of *The Unnamable* is all waiting.

For Molloy, the quest proper begins "on a road remarkably bare" (9). Molloy sees two strangers meet and greet each other on this white road, with the sea and the "waning sky" beyond them. He empathizes with one of these strangers, picturing him concerned not only with the outer but with the inner land-scape, again using Eliot's words: "What shall I do? What shall I do? (11; cf. *The Waste Land*, line 131 "What shall I do now? What shall I do?"). He is compassionate for the state of this unknown man, "abroad alone, by unknown ways, in the gather-ing night"[9] (11). The whole scene has a dreamlike, mythic qual-ity, which sets the stage appropriately for the mythic quest, much as Langland's dream of the field of folk enhances the opening mood of *Piers the Ploughman*. Molloy himself is crouched, "like Belacqua, or Sordello"[10] (12) behind a rock. The landscape has been called purgatorial, because it is neither light nor dark, but this is not precisely accurate. In the *Purgato-rio* the sun (representing the light of God) rises and sets, and there is no climbing up the Mount of Purgatory at night. The notion of Purgatory as always crepuscular is a modern one, deriving from Eliot's *The Waste Land*, with an assist from Beck-ett in the trilogy.

The importance of Belacqua as Beckett's representative fig-ure has been established and stressed by many critics, for ex-ample, Fletcher and Harvey. Just as Eliot in *The Waste Land* speaks through the *persona* of Dante's Arnaut Daniel ("be mind-ful of my pain") so Beckett (or Molloy) speaks through the *persona* of Belacqua, whose name also begins with "B" and whose ironic tone is eminently suited to Beckett. Belacqua's sin, of course, was indolence or *akedia*, the central sin in the *Purga-torio* and also in *The Waste Land*. Langland, too, in an autobio-graphical passage in *Piers the Ploughman*, portrays himself as indolent and indifferent: "I was fond of an easy life, and had nothing better to do than drink and sleep. And . . . I roamed along content with the world" (C-text). Condemnation of spiri-tual laxness is very much in the classic Christian tradition; for example, there are many poems by George Herbert on "Em-ployment," in which he bewails his sloth and speaks of man's "faint desire for God." In the special Beckett issue of *New The-*

---

[9]Mr. Beckett has informed me that this strikingly cadenced phrase is without literary reference as far as he is aware. It is perhaps only coincidence that it echoes a line from Hymn 553 in the Episcopal Hymnal, verse 4: "Go forward, Christian soldier/ Fear not the gather-ing night."

[10]See Purgatorio, Canto IV.

atre Magazine, Beckett's friend Calder says, "But Beckett thinks of himself as idle. He presents himself as idle in his work" (17).

It is useless to speculate who the two strangers (called "A" and "C") are; Molloy confuses them, and their appearance is more a function of setting than of plot. There may, however, be some subliminal contrast intended with Dante and Virgil, who do notice Belacqua and speak to him, whereas the passersby ignore Molloy-Belacqua, who wants desperately to run in panic and loneliness after one of the two men and speak to him. Molloy pictures the passerby responding courteously enough but knows that the latter will disengage himself and go on. He contemplates the other man and wonders about him. Then his mind drifts to his hat, attached to his coat by an elastic through the buttonhole, and to his crutches. These possessions are dear to him, but he says, "I shall perhaps one day throw them away" (17). This is a first reference to the stripping process essential to the mystic encounter. He points out that he is "on the top, or on the slopes, of some considerable eminence" (17) which again correlates with the Mount of Purgatory in Dante's *Divine Comedy,* and he questions, "I, what was I doing there, and why come? These are things that we shall try and discover" (17). Somewhat irrelevantly, he points out that "in my night there is no moon, and if it happens that I speak of the stars it is by mistake" (18). Since Dante specifically points out the stars that shine in Purgatory, this very pointed reference by Beckett establishes the crepuscular nature of modern man's purgatory. Molloy continues, "And so at last I came out of that distant night, divided between the murmurs of my little world, its dutiful confusions, and those so different (so different?) of all that between two suns abides and passes away" (18), probably an allusion to the passage in Ecclesiastes 1:4: "One generation passeth away and another generation cometh: but the earth abideth forever."

Molloy wakes late in the morning, hears "the angelus, recalling the incarnation, shortly after" (19), and sets off on his journey, ostensibly to see his mother, but in fact to attain some enlightenment as to the condition of man in relation to the four last things.

As Molloy leaves his mount, he refers to it as "this earthly paradise" (20), a phrase which at first glance appears again to be merely irony, but which also connotes the whole Belacqua-Dante-Purgatory ambience. He refers to his journey as "that unreal journey" (21), a phrase which recalls Eliot's "unreal city" (*The Waste Land*, l. 60). Rather than connoting schizophrenia (*pace* Barnard), the phrase implies that the quest is one of the spirit.

Molloy discusses his father and mother in highly unflattering terms. His father's name is Dan—an interesting choice, for Dan was Jacob's son, not by his wife but by his handmaid, and therefore is somewhat of an outcast. According to the *Jewish Encyclopedia,* Dan is regarded in Jewish mythology as associated with the devil, and the insignia of the tribe of Dan was the serpent. Molloy is a paradigm of man in general, as all Beckett's M–characters are; thus the fatherhood of Dan connotes man's fallen state. The name Dan, being from the Old Testament, signifies Judaism, whereas Molloy's mother's name, Mag or Magdalen, is related to Christianity. Molloy therefore is the child of Judaism and Christianity.

Molloy's attitude to his mother is hostile, and she is described in tones of repulsion. He communicates with her by knocking on her skull, as the protagonists do in *How It Is.* Although one is horrified by the graphic description of Mag's senile state and the brutality of Molloy's attempts at communication, these can be seen on one level as a way of breaking through our unfeeling condition and of rendering vividly the ugliness of senescent old people and the difficulty we find in communicating with them. Honest persons will see these descriptions as metaphors for the blandly brutal behavior which is perfectly evident in homes and hospitals. However, on the allegorical level they can be seen as the difficulty of Molloy (man) in communicating with his Christian antecedents—just as in waiting for Godot Vladimir and Estragon have trouble remembering their Christian culture.

At any rate, Molloy pushes on and comes to the city. " . . . the ways into and of course out of this town are narrow and darkened by enormous vaults, without exception. It is a good rule and I observe it religiously . . . " (25), the rule being that on approaching the city one must dismount and/or slow down. "Thus we cleared these difficult straits" (25). (See Matt. 7:14, "Strait is the gate, and narrow is the way.") Can it be that this good rule, which he observes "religiously," is the first step on the negative way: to detach oneself gradually from the cares and possessions of every-day life? Molloy next has a preliminary skirmish with the pharisaical guardians of law and order. Yet in spite of this harassment, here occurs the first of many passages throughout the trilogy which intimate mystical experiences:

> I felt the faces turning to look after us, calm faces and joyful faces, faces of men, of women and of children. I seemed to hear, at a certain moment, a distant music . . . . Forgetful of my mother, set free from the act, merged in this alien hour, saying, Respite, respite. (26–27)

The passage indicates several attributes of the mystical experience—unity with others ("I felt the faces turning to look after us, calm faces and joyful faces, faces of men, of women and of children"), peace and detachment ("Set free from the act"). According to W. H. Auden in a description of nature-mysticism in *The Protestant Mystics:* "Occasionally human figures are involved, but if so, they are invariably . . . strangers to the subject . . . passersby, beggars, or the like, of whom he has no personal knowledge. The basic experience is an overwhelming conviction that the objects confronting him have a numimous significance and importance, that the existence of everything he is aware of is holy" (13).

It is noon, the hour of the angelus, "recalling the incarnation," as the narrator says. But according to Goodridge in his edition of *Piers the Ploughman,* " . . . midday is traditionally the time when the Devil . . . tries a man most severely . . . . Moreover, it was at the time of the 'greatest light' that the world was plunged into darkness" (at the crucifixion) (275). It is not surprising, then, that Molloy appears before his accusers and is tormented in a scene somewhat suggesting Christ before the Sanhedrin or before Pilate. Among those critics who have admitted Beckett's preoccupation with Christianity, most have seen his view of Christ as one which excludes or even perhaps precludes his divinity and rather stresses his humanity as a paradigm of all suffering humanity.

It is interesting to note that Molloy gives his mother's address as "by the shambles" (28). (Similarly, the home Celia finds for Murphy is near the Metropolitan Cattle Market.) Symbolically, this could refer to the brutality of all human life. But, pushing the symbol to the ultimate, we remember the shambles in the Jewish temple was close to the altar, and one can perhaps see this as an allusion to the Jewish roots of Christian tradition ("my mother").

In the guardroom, a woman "social worker" offers Molloy bread and tea, here, as they are in Joyce's *A Portrait of the Artist as a Young Man* (Chapter V), an ironic analogue to the Eucharist. But Molloy throws the food against the wall. Perhaps this is a symbolic rejection of institutionalized communion with the divine. However, I find it more likely related to a comment of Simone Weil's in *Waiting for God:* "If the gift is rightly given and rightly received the passing of a morsel of bread from one man to another is something like a real communion" (96). Presumably, the gift is not here rightly given, although later on Molloy (or someone resembling Molloy) accepts a gift of bread from Moran, a frightful sinner but also a quester. Whatever the theology of Molloy's action in rejecting the social worker's bread and tea, he is set free without penalty, to his surprise and ours. He speculates that he has "a friend at Court" (31), and that "to apply the letter of the law to a creature like me" (31) is difficult. This recalls Paul's statement that "the letter killeth, but the spirit giveth life" (2 Cor. 3:6), a pregnant saying in the context of police courts, accusations, and slaughter-houses.

Molloy has been arrested because his preferred position on the bicycle, with his head down on his arms, sets a deplorable example to the people, who "need to be encouraged in their bitter toil" (31). Is it too much to suppose this a glancing reference to those readers and critics much distressed by Beckett's own supposed pessimism? Be that as it may. A *miserere* follows, in which Molloy expresses the torment and misery of his passion, a "passion without form or stations," again an allusion to Christ's passion and the stations of the cross (33). Then seeing his shadow on the wall he plays, "gesticulating, waving my hat, moving my bicycle to and fro before me, blowing the horn, watching the wall" (33). He refers to this as "the shadow" and complains that in the end it is no better than the substance; in other words, art is playing with shadows.

At any rate, off he goes, and next encounters little donkeys, pulling a barge full of nails and timber, "on the way to some

carpenter I suppose" (34). The conjunction of nails, timber and
carpenter certainly reinforces the Christian content of Molloy.[11]
The boatman pulling the barge has a long white beard. One can
associate the boatman and the canal with the Styx (Molloy is
going to die a spiritual death), or the long white beard with the
anthropomorphic Judaic god in Revelation 1:14–16 or as drawn
by Michelangelo and Blake. "The horizon was burning with sul-
phur and phosphorus, it was there I was bound" (34) is an obvious reference to hell. Instead of proceeding, Molloy lies down in
the ditch, in the attitude of the crucifixion, under a hawthorn,
traditionally regarded as the plant from which Christ's crown of
thorns was made. It would be a mistake to regard this symbolic
death as a literal one. He is dying to the world, for he says of
himself, "It is not you who are dead, but all the others" (35). He
hears the "howl resolving all" (35), perhaps a reference to the
groan of the whole earth at the crucifixion, and asks ironically
"Where are the famous flies?" (35), an allusion to Sartre's *The
Flies*. He continues: "The night in the ditch, and perfect silence,
and behind my closed lids the little night and its little lights, faint
at first, then flaming and extinguished, now ravening, now fed,
as fire by filth and martyrs" (36).

He wakes to see a shepherd going by with a flock, and is
afflicted with dreadful doubts, wondering which lambs are des-
tined for slaughter.[12] He reminds himself that he must again
set out for his mother, although he is not sure which is the
right road. The thought disturbs him, "like all recall to life"

---

[11]In the Samuel Beckett Special Issue of *New Theatre Magazine* Martin Esslin tells an anecdote about Jack MacGowran reading in Beckett's
presence a poem by Beckett in which "there is a line about the barges
in the canal by the Guinness Brewery, laden with nails and timber,
with timber and nails—I can't recall it in detail. Jack was reading this
and he (Beckett) said, 'Oh no, no, no, not just nails and timber; *nails
and timber*—that's the cross'" (14). Esslin went on to say that he
thought they (other panelists) should talk about this a bit: "this curious
co-existence of Christian imagery also in *Waiting for Godot*, the thieves
and the cross—and at the same time this rejection of any metaphysical
belief of this kind" (14).

[12]Note that in *Purgatorio*, Canto III, Dante sees the souls of the
Late-Repentant as a flock of sheep. The image of the flock of sheep is
used again by Beckett in the Moran section of *Molloy* in a way which
strikingly recalls Dante's use.

(40), that is, true life as opposed to merely going through the outward motions. This phrase, like so much in *Molloy,* reminds us of Eliot: "April is the cruelest month," and "This birth was hard and bitter agony for us." His bicycle runs over a dog, but the woman who owns the dog is not angry, because the dog was old and decrepit. Her name is Sophia Loy or Lousse. So deftly and quickly does Beckett shift to calling her "Lousse" (Louse? Soul?) that we neglect to observe that her name is first given as Sophia (Wisdom) Loy. Sophia, the Divine Wisdom, is a concept pervading the early church, especially but not exclusively in the Eastern branch. Alan Watts makes some enlightening comments on Sophia in his *Myth and Ritual in Christianity* (90, 102). "Loy" has been explicated by Ruby Cohn as "law." Further investigation reveals that "loy" or "loi" is the root of a number of Old French words whose connotations are loyalty or constancy. The *Oxford Dictionary of English Etymology* shows the French *loyaute* and English *loyal* as coming from the Old French *leial* (English *leal*). I, therefore, would paraphrase the woman's name as Wisdom Faith, or Wisdom Constancy. Physically, Sophia is a shadowy character, one of the three women in the trilogy, one in each book, not described in repulsive detail. The significance of the tree and the garden here is probably the same as it is in *Waiting for Godot,* which I discuss in a later chapter. In the course of digging a grave for the dog, which is difficult for him with his stiff leg, Molloy is led to consider the state of his testicles, and quotes Leopardi ("A se stesso,"*Canti,* XXVIII):[13] "non che la spema il desiderio" (47)—a phrase which Beckett quoted also in his essay on Proust, indicating the stress he places on ablation of desire rather than its satisfaction.

At Lousse's, his hat is taken away, then the rest of his clothing, and he is shaven. In other words, he is being stripped preparatory to beginning the process of detachment from the world. He speaks of cutting off his balls, which "got in his way," but he is not quite ready for that yet. He talks about all the disciplines, 'ologies and 'isms of mankind, and concludes, in this House of Wisdom, that they are all useless. "What I liked in anthropology," he says, "was its inexhaustible faculty of negation, its relentless definition of man, as though he were no

---

[13]See L. Harvey, *Samuel Beckett: Poet and Critic,* 188, 189.

better than God, in terms of what he is not" (52). Unless he is theologically experienced, the reader may see this as simple irony against God and man, not knowing that in patristic theology, God *is* apprehended by His negative attributes. For example, E. Herman in *The Meaning and Value of Mysticism,* says, "This negative way of approach to God is really the way of analogy reversed. It proceeds upon the assumption that, since the infinite is the complete antithesis of the finite, *everything* that can be affirmed of man must logically be denied of God who can only be described by negative" (299). Beckett's irony accomplishes the same end as "the way of analogy reversed." Elmer O'Brien's *Varieties of Mystic Experience* gives in the section on the Pseudo-Dionysius an exhaustive list of the negative attributes of God:

> He is
>> not soul or intelligence,
>> not imagination or conjecture or reason or under-
>>> standing,
>> not word, not intellection,
>> not said, not thought,
>> not number, not order,
>> not magnitude, not littleness,
>> not likeness, not unlikeness,
>> not similarity, not dissimilarity,
>> not unmoving, not moved,
>> not powerful, not power,
>> not light,
>> not living, not life,
>> not essence,
>> not eon, not time,
>> not understandable,
>> not knowledge, not truth,
>> not kingship, not wisdom,
>> not one, not unity,
>> not deity,
>> not goodness,
>> not spirit (as we know spirit),
>> not filiation,
>> not paternity,

> not anything known by us or by anyone among us,
> not a nonbeing,
> not a being,
> not known, as He is, by beings,
> not knower of beings as they are,
> not definable,
> *not nameable,* [Italics mine]
> not knowable,
> not dark, not light,
> not untrue, not true,
> not affirmable, not deniable

Even so, Beckett's statement may still appear to be irony at the expense of man, unless one realizes that to attain their object, Pure Being, or God, the mystics must go through a state of negativity, of nothingness.

Soon appears the third long mystical passage full of paradoxical expressions, a description of a soundless, timeless place, with haunting echoes of T. S. Eliot:

> I listen and the voice is of a world collapsing endlessly, a frozen world, under a faint untroubled sky, enough to see by, yes, and frozen too. And I hear it murmur that all wilts and yields as if loaded down, but here there are no loads, and the ground too, unfit for loads, and the light too, down towards an end it seems can never come. For what possible end to these wastes where true light never was, nor any upright thing, nor any true foundation, but only these leaning things, forever lapsing and crumbling away, beneath a sky without memory of morning or hope of night. (53)

Compare with Eliot's lines (*Burnt Norton,* III):

> Here is a place of disaffection
> Time before and after
> In a dim light: neither daylight
> Investing form with lucid stillness
> Turning shadow into transient beauty
> With slow rotation suggesting permanence
> Nor darkness to purify the soul

These two descriptions of what is often in modern criticism called the purgatorial world are obviously similar and equally obviously descriptions of a dead land, a wasteland, which hardly resembles the strenuous sunlit purgatory of Dante's imagination. Rather, this gray world is the world at the beginning of the negative way, when the soul has realized the necessity of the journey away from the world. The similarity to Eliot's lines is further emphasized by the fact that earlier, Molloy has talked about his phenomenal capacity to fart (39), which evokes Eliot's "eructation of unhealthy souls." In addition, the phrase "no thunder can deliver me" (54) reminds us that in Eliot's *The Waste Land* God finally spoke through the thunder.

Prior to the vision of the gray world, he has had a sudden vision of the moon, which startles and worries him, because his nights are moonless usually, and he takes this as a sign that he should immediately leave Lousse's house and again start on the quest for his mother. Molloy obtains his clothes, his bicycle, and his other possessions and tries to go away. He is halted in the garden by Lousse, who attempts to induce him to stay. Although the suggestion that he stay in the House of Wisdom is enormously appealing, he is ambivalent. Lousse is "in the garden, fussing around the grave. . . . She was taking advantage of the cool of the evening" (62). Since the grave is at the foot of the tree where the dog lies buried, the cluster of associations is one familiar from *Waiting for Godot* (see chapter VII). Sophia (Wisdom) is in the garden where stood the Tree of Life, where God used to come in the cool of the day, according to the King James Version of the Bible. As Lousse attempts to persuade him, he notes the smell of spike-lavender and comments upon it for several lines. Spike-lavender does actually grow in the British Isles, but possibly the subliminal association with spikenard (Mark 14:3, John 12:3) is intended here. Spikenard is the expensive ointment used by Mary Magdalene to anoint Christ.

In the fourth mystical passage, which follows immediately upon the mention of the spike-lavender, he has a sensation of oneness:

> And there was another noise, that of my life become the life of this garden as it rode the earth of deeps and wilder-

nesses. Yes, there were times when I forgot not only who I was, but that I was, forgot to be. Then I was no longer that sealed jar to which I owed my being so well preserved, but a wall gave way and I filled with roots and tame stems for example, stakes long since dead and ready for burning, the recess of night and the imminence of dawn, and then the labour of the planet rolling eager into winter, winter would rid it of these contemptible scabs. (65)

This intuition of oneness with created things, like all the others so far, is not the true mystical experience; it is only a glimpse of it, such as any sensitive pantheist might have. It is to be understood, as Dom Cuthbert Butler says, "that there are phases and stages of mysticism that fall short of the supreme experiences" (5).

In contemplating why he did not leave Lousse's immediately, although he wanted to and intended to, Molloy refers to "Geulincx, dead young, who left me free, on the black boat of Ulysses, to crawl towards the East, along the deck" (68). The reference to Geulincx's metaphor of the crawling man on the ship is usually taken to indicate Beckett's pessimistic view of man's lack of freedom. However, an extreme emphasis on God's omnipotence in contrast to man's impotence is characteristic of mysticism. Otto says: "To the creature then is denied . . . true reality and complete being, and all existence and fullness of being is ascribed to the absolute entity, who alone really is" (90), and he states that this sequence of ideas is found in particularly explicit form in the mysticism of Geulincx and the Occasionalists.[14] As Otto explains, " . . . here the futility of one's own choice, there the will that ordains all, determines all" (89).

But this concept of man's limited freedom is neither the modern determinist, reductionist view, nor yet the Calvinist sense of the predestined elect. Rather, it is the mystic's sense

[14]Occasionalism is a philosophic theory devised in the seventeenth century by Guelincx and Malebranche to counter Descartes's dualism of mind and matter. The Occasionalists deny causality and assert that all events are directly the result of God's will. For the influence of Geulincx on Beckett, see John Fletcher, *Samuel Beckett's Art,* pp. 131–134, or John Pilling, *Samuel Beckett,* p.115.

that nothing in all the world matters but God, and therefore no action that is not taken to that End is worth anything. In any case, busy actions do not achieve union with God, but only a silent waiting can. The importance of this passive "waiting" cannot be stressed too strongly, particularly in an era when mankind has been conditioned to pragmatic activism, to feeling that a "program" will solve and save. But it must be emphasized that this kind of passivity does not imply an ultimate futility, because beyond it there is always the Divine, and the soul is waiting to be seized or called by the Divine. To identify Geulincx's "fatalism" or that of any other Christian with nihilism or futility is to make a most horrendous and basic error. Although all the Western Christian mystics have expressed a similar view of man's limited area of free will, it is very vividly and concretely expressed by Simone Weil in the first letter in *Waiting for God:*

> In this domain everything which comes about is in accordance with the will of God, without any exception. . . . In other words, we must feel the reality and presence of God through all external things, without exception, as clearly as our hand feels the substance of paper through the penholder and the nib. (43–44)

The secular-minded reader may question why the references to Geulincx or the seeming analogies to Weil are not ironic. They may be, as far as Beckett's own personal life is concerned. But in the novel, Molloy does not leave Lousse's until a little voice tells him to. In the first chapter, letter three, of Simone Weil's *Waiting for God*, she says: "It seems to me as though something were telling me to go" (59), and almost immediately thereafter, she talks about the two thieves on either side of Christ, saying, "Of all the beings other than Christ of whom the Gospel tells us, the good thief is by far the one I most envy" (26). It is a striking coincidence that within a few pages Molloy is considering the knife-rest with its two crosses, after he has left the house of Wisdom and Faith.

Molloy describes the bread and wine he receives to eat at Lousse's house: "I never had to call for it," he says (73), and declares that the "food" (communion?) would appear at the most unsuspected times and places. Sometimes he omitted to eat, and he refers to both acts and omissions as "eudemonistic slop," a term which refers to a system of ethics that evaluates the morality of actions in terms of their capacity to produce happiness—Bentham's hedonistic calculus, in other words. Molloy does point out, however, that at Lousse's (the House of Faith and Wisdom) he at least did not become worse in health and developed no new ailments.

With seeming irrelevance, there appears a long and disgusting reminiscence of Molloy's sexual relations with one Ruth or Edith. It seems likely that this sexual reminiscence is a remote parallel to Dante's dream of the Siren in the *Purgatorio*, just as Molloy's inactivity at Lousse's remotely parallels the sin of sloth or *akedia* in the same book. As Molloy discusses his relationship with Ruth-Edith, he constantly and ironically uses the word "love." In Dante's theology and in classical theology generally, sexual relationships *per se*, regarded as mere mechanics, are a perversion of love, and it is undoubtedly this sense of things which Beckett is expressing. Dante's Siren is described in the same kind of revolting imagery: "a stuttering crone,/ squint-eyed, club-footed, both her hands deformed,/ and her complexion like a white-washed stone" (*Purgatorio*, Canto XIX, ll.7–9). When Virgil lays bare "all of her front, her loins, and her foul belly," Dante is "sick with the stench that rose from there." The disgusting detail and the sense of nausea are exactly comparable to those of Beckett's Molloy.[15]

Another analogy to the use of physically revolting imagery to indicate the nature of concupiscence would be Eliot's copulating couples in *The Waste Land*. However, although Eliot is clinically blunt about sexuality, it remains for the low-church Protestant Beckett to give the most distasteful and revolting expression possible of this theme. In this he is closer to his compatriot Swift than to Eliot or Dante. But whatever the degree of disgust, an emphasis on the filthy, obscene, or scatalogical is a classical Christian technique for emphasizing the discrepancy between the perfection and transcendence of the Absolute and the imperfection and fallibility of the mortal. All

---

[15]See also Herbert's "Home": "What is this woman-kinde which I can wink/ Into a blacknesse and distaste?" and Milton's description of the "Beavie of Fair Women" who seduce the sober sons of men in *Paradise Lost*, Book XI.

the thinkers and writers favored by Beckett—St. Augustine, Dante, Bunyan, Pascal, Geulincx, Swift, Joyce, Eliot—have in one way or another used this technique.

Lousse's house and garden have another "strait gate," a little wicket gate (as also in Beckett's *Watt*), opening on a road, a narrow gate that is never locked. It is noteworthy that the wicket gate, whose prototype is in the New Testament, appears in Langland's *Piers the Ploughman* (Passus I, 1.6), in Bunyan's *Pilgrim's Progress*, and in Herbert's poem "Holy Baptism," as well as in the trilogy. Convinced that Sophia Lousse is poisoning him (either because he is not ready to accept Wisdom or because for him Wisdom, although a good in itself, blocks the intuition of the Divine), Molloy gets his crutches and goes, afraid that if he lingers, he will cease hearing "the small voice saying, Get out of here. . . . Outside in the road the wind was blowing. Not knowing where I was nor consequently what way I ought to go I went with the wind. And when, well slung between my crutches, I took off, then I felt it helping me, that little wind blowing from what quarter I could not tell" (80). So much mention of the wind is significant. Down through the ages, the wind or stirring of the air has always been a symbol for the Divine; it is found preeminently in the Pentecost story (Acts 2:2): "And suddenly there came a sound from heaven as of a rushing mighty wind, and it filled all the house where they were sitting." A more relevant reference is probably John 3:8: "The wind bloweth where it listeth, and thou hearest the sound thereof, but canst not tell whence it cometh, and whither it goeth; so is everyone that is born of the Spirit."

Searching for shelter, Molloy enters a blind alley, whose nooks (referred to as "alcoves" and "chapels") are littered with rubbish. He is tempted to settle down there, but instead, after a half-hearted attempt at suicide, he goes on. If the House of Wisdom and Faith could symbolically represent the classical Christianity of pre-Reformation Catholicism, might these blind alleys represent the various Protestantisms of which Beckett spoke so scathingly to Tom Driver?

Although it is raining, he notes that he is headed in the direction of the sun (as Dante and Virgil travel toward the sun, symbolizing the divine, in the *Purgatorio*). He recalls the knife-rest he had stolen from Lousse with its "two crosses, joined, at their points of intersection by a bar" (85). He could never bring himself to sell it, and would look at it from time to time; it even inspired him "with a kind of veneration" (85). The knife-rest's two crosses should be associated with the two thieves crucified on either side of Christ, those two thieves mentioned in the now-famous sentence by St. Augustine, of which Beckett declares he admires the shape, so Alan Schneider tells us in "Waiting for Beckett" in the *Chelsea Review*, No. 2 (1958): "Do not despair, one of the thieves was saved; do not presume, one of the thieves was damned." The allusion is to the possibility of salvation, a loaded word whose legalistic and Calvinistic connotations are extremely inappropriate for either Molloy or Beckett. Possibility of union with the divine would be a more suitable way of putting it ("Today thou shalt be with me in Paradise"). It is interesting to note that the question of the two thieves is a point of argument in the B-text of *Piers the Ploughman*. In Passus X Langland argues that baptism and good works are unnecessary to salvation because the repentant thief was saved "before St. John the Baptist or Adam or Isaiah or any of the prophets who had lain in hell for hundreds of years. And so a robber was ransomed sooner than all the others, and was brought to perpetual bliss without purgatory or penance." In reply, Imagination points out that the thief was repentant and turned to Christ freely, but that nevertheless his reward was not the same as that of the saints: ". . . the thief was placed in Paradise—lounging at ease in the lowest reaches of Heaven. . . . And if you ask why one of the crucified thieves accepted the Faith, rather than the other, not all the clergy of Christ could give you an answer. 'Whatsoever the Lord pleased, that did He.'" There follows in *Piers* a beautiful passage in which Imagination explains that God is incomprehensible to Reason alone. Another suggestive point is that the two thieves (and the two qualities—presumption and despair) occur also in the *Pensées* (Nos. 75, 610, 677) and also , as I have mentioned, in Simone Weil's *Waiting for God* (59). If these parallels do not prove influence, they at any rate indicate similar preoccupations. Significantly, Beckett also referred to the two thieves in *More Pricks than Kicks*, and more importantly, in the interview with Tom Driver.

The rest of page 85, disregarding some irrelevancies and

interruptions, is a paean to the kind of un-anxious, uncaring acceptance which is the aim of true Christianity no less than of Buddhism. Molloy indicates that the thought of the knife-rest in his pocket induces him to think less about his mother and what the name of the town is. Unpurposefully and peacefully, he leaves the town, noting as he does so that the setting sun is emitting "living tongues of fire" (87). This phrase recalls the epiphany at Pentecost in the upper room, especially when one associates it with the earlier reference to the wind. In a sudden reference to his state at the time of writing, Molloy comments that he is still detached from all earthly and worldly cares ("And the confines of my room, of my bed, of my body, are as remote from me as were those of my region, in the days of my splendour" [88]). As he swings along in the dark, he reminds himself that "they," the watchmen and bullies, usually do not persecute him too much in the night, leaving that to the "technicians." The sense of the passage and the use of the word "watchmen" link Molloy with Kafka's hunger artist, also a spiritual quester, who is scrutinized by the "butchers." Then comes another digression, this one the famous "sucking-stone" routine, at which one does not know whether to laugh or to weep; it is a magnificent burlesque of all obsessive ratiocinative activity, the kind of activity from which Molloy has very nearly succeeded in freeing himself. At the end of the soliloquy, he carelessly throws away all but one of the stones, indicating he is surrendering this kind of compulsive behavior.

With his leg giving him considerable difficulty, Molloy presses on through a swamp which reminds us of the Slough of Despond in *The Pilgrim's Progress*. But just as Dante and Virgil in the *Purgatorio* are unable to climb once the Divine Illumination has departed for the day, so Molloy progresses slowly and with enormous difficulty. He encounters a charcoal burner, vaguely surrounded by smoke, a kind of devil-figure who has lived all his life in the forest. Molloy kills this person in a peculiarly brutal and sinister way. What is one to say about this perverse murder, except to note that it had apparently been preceded by an equally perverse proposition? "He was all over me, begging me to share his hut, believe it or not . . . sick with solitude probably" (113). It is noteworthy that in the *Purgatorio*, Canto XVII, the Ledge of the Wrathful is approached through clouds of smoke, just as Molloy sees smoke in the forest and says, "That's something that never escapes me, smoke." Similarly, in Canto XVII, Dante sees three examples of murder by the wrathful.

Molloy continues in a circle, just as the pilgrims in the *Divine Comedy* do. He feels like staying in the forest (again, *akedia*), but some "imperative" insists that he try to find his way out of it. The "voice" even gives him a solemn warning in Latin: "Nimis sero" (117), a warning taken from Lucretius ("Perhaps it is already too late when we reach the end"), clearly another reference to "the last things." He uses Christ's phrase "Yet a little while" (John 7:33) (118), perhaps meaning that in a little while he will return to his "mother" or to the quest, but his difficulty in walking increases to the point of almost stopping him from proceeding. He mentions ironically that he does not hear the "celebrated" forest murmurs (celebrated either in *Purgatorio*, Canto XXVII, ll.17–18, or in Wagner's *Siegfried*). Instead he hears a gong, an image which calls to mind the Sanctus bell sounding at the elevation of the host during the Mass, Beckett's supposed Protestantism, existentialism, or atheism notwithstanding. (It should be borne in mind that at roughly the comparable point in the *Purgatorio*, the questers encounter the heavenly pageant [*Purgatorio*, Canto XXIX], with the Griffon representing Christ.) Crawling on his belly ("I am a worm and no man," Psalm 22; "My soul cleaves to the dust," Psalm 119), Molloy soon after sees "the light, the light of the plain" (122), and then the towers and steeples of a town, and finally he enters the last of the mystical states described in *Molloy:*

> It must have been spring, a morning in spring. I thought I heard birds, skylarks perhaps. I had not heard a bird for a long time. How was it that I had not heard any in the forest? Nor seen any. . . . I saw the sheep again. Or so I say now. I did not fret, other scenes of my life came back to me. There seemed to be rain, then sunshine, turn about. Real spring weather. I longed to go back into the forest. Oh not a real longing. Molloy could stay, where he happened to be. (123–124)

Arranged in lines, the prose appears to be poetry. As in Eliot's work, and in Christian mythology and symbology generally, the bird symbolizes the divine. Associated with the sheep, the spring time of hope and resurrection, and Molloy's freedom from anxiety, this experience of Molloy's appears to be a mystical experience of communion with the divine.

In spite of its strangeness and occasional savagery, this portion of *Molloy* is a beautiful work, haunting with hints of spiritual enlightenment. *Molloy* is the story of a soul already advanced on the "way," although he is not as yet sufficiently detached, sufficiently adept at the negation of all, to arrive at the Dark Night which will lead into all light.

A very different personality from the gentle, dreamy, ironic Molloy, Moran is authoritarian, legalistic, preoccupied with rules, regulations, and status. He talks constantly about religion, but he might as well be talking about the regulations and liturgy of the police department or the secret service. Yet his story too is a religious allegory—the story of a man who, like Molloy, goes on a quest and discards his possessions. As the story opens, he is summoned by a messenger named Gaber, who comes from one Youdi. John Fletcher has already pointed out that Youdi is a variant of Yahweh, and that Gaber is derived from Gabriel. Leo Baeck states in *Judaism and Christianity* that the word "gaber or geber" means "son of man" (26). According to Baeck,". . . the book of Daniel lends our words [son of man] . . . a special connotation. It tells of beings who belong to the world above, yet look like men . . . Daniel, too, says, 'Behold, there stood before me as the appearance of a man'—kemar gaber. . . . Always a being from above is meant, one of those with human appearance dwelling up there" (26). Actually, Beckett himself gives us the clue; on page 145 he states: "Gaber was a messenger," and he emphasizes that Gaber is totally innocent of the message he delivers. In Judaism, angels, the messengers of God, often appear in human form. Simone Weil speaks of such a messenger in *Waiting for God.* In her case the "messenger" introduced her to the seventeenth-century English metaphysical poets, including George Herbert. It was while she was reciting Herbert's "Love" that "Christ himself came down and took possession of" Simone Weil (68–69).

It is thus obvious that Moran's call is a divine call to break out of his "futile, anxious life" (167) and enter upon the "way":

It was then the unheard of sight was to be seen of Moran making ready to go without knowing where he was going, having consulted neither map nor timetable, considered neither itinerary nor halts, heedless of the weather outlook, with only the vaguest notion of the outfit he would need, the time the expedition was likely to take, the money he would require and even the very nature of the work to be done and consequently the means to be employed. (169)

Both Fletcher and Ruby Cohn, among many others, have summarized the "Moran" section so well that it is not necessary to repeat every detail, particularly when Moran's story is so much more "realistic" than that of Molloy. However, it is interesting to note that his servant is called Martha, and remembering the petty, bustling Martha who is contrasted with the silent listening Mary in the story of Christ's visit to Lazarus, this name seems an appropriate one for a servant of the literal and egotistical Moran. Moran's reluctance to take his son along with him, as instructed by Gaber, presents a parody of the Abraham-Isaac story—that story which plays such an important part in the existential faith of Kierkegaard. The parallel is not complete, however, for Moran Junior is not to be sacrificed; instead his father is to go through some strange and transforming experiences. The first of these experiences is perhaps the dim recognition that the Molloy he is going out to seek at Gaber's behest is part of himself: "He had only to rise up within me for me to be filled with panting" (154). "Between the Molloy I stalked within me thus and the true Molloy, after whom I was so soon to be in full cry, over hill and dale, the resemblance cannot have been great" (157). Actually, as Beckett makes clear, the resemblance is not of great importance in the story. "For what I was doing I was doing neither for Molloy, who mattered nothing to me, nor for myself, of whom I despaired, but on behalf of a cause which, while having need of us to be accomplished, was in its essence anonymous, and would subsist, haunting the minds of men, when its miserable artisans should be no more" (156–157). These poetic lines evoke the mythic quality so striking in this trilogy, and make one wonder if perhaps Moran is to Molloy as Judas was to Christ. The suppressed Molloy within Moran parallels Judas' simultaneous wish to be one of Christ's followers and his rebellion against his own commitment. With these analogies in mind, one can hardly repress a grin at realizing that the gong (Sanctus bell?) also sounds for Moran as it did for Molloy, and that he sits down to a quasi-communion supper of soup and hardly-to-be-credited "shepherd's pie," the pie of the "good shepherd" who actually appears to both Molloy and Moran and who symbolizes God or Christ as he does in the New Testament. The staggering effrontery of such a joke leaves one dazed, thinking only how Joyce would have loved it.

Moran's son is ill, and for a moment Moran contemplates using that as an excuse not to go on the quest. But only for a moment: "it was not for nothing I had studied the old testament" (162). Angrily he gives his son an enema, reflecting that "He [Youdi] asked for a report he'll get his report" (164). Dressed outlandishly, and with his hat, like Molloy's, attached to his buttonhole by an elastic, Moran leads his son through the by now familiar wicket gate: "I had left, accompanied by my son, in accordance with instructions received" (180). But Moran's reactions are ambivalent; he is just beginning to learn to listen to the "voices":

> Yes, it is rather an ambiguous voice and not always easy to follow, in its reasonings and decrees. But I follow it none the less, more or less, I follow it in this sense, that I know what it means, and in this sense, that I do what it tells me. And I do not think there are many voices of which as much may be said. And I feel I shall follow it from this day forth, no matter what it commands. And when it ceases, leaving me in doubt and darkness, I shall wait for it to come back, and do nothing. . . . (pp. 180–81)

When Moran and his son emerge through the wicket gate, they walk along a lane which is *below* the graveyard, so that in effect they are "faring below the dead" (184), or in other words they are making the classical descent into hell.[16] Molloy's story starts in a strange quasi-Purgatorio, Moran's begins like

---

[16]Or, in Jungian terms, the descent into the unconscious; Beckett's terms of reference, however, seem blessedly free of psychological or psychoanalytic jargon or imagery.

Dante's, in hell, thus producing the impression that all spiritual life is a cycle revolving around the different stages of separation from, or approximation to, the Divine. Moran says: 'Sometimes I smiled, as if I were dead already" (185). And later, "Things steal back into position for the day, take their stand, sham dead" (191).

Like Molloy's, his legs give him trouble, and he is reduced to crawling. He wants a bicycle (symbol of Cartesian reason), and sends his son for a second-hand one. As his son leaves, Moran plucks a bough from a tree in a sudden fury and hurls it after him. Immediately afterwards he masturbates. Again we can see a kind of loose parallel to the various sins illustrated by Dante in the *Purgatorio*—hypocrisy at the beginning of the story, wrath, lust, and so on. The breaking of the bough may be a symbolic gesture intended to recall for us Aeneas' descent into Hades and his breaking of the golden bough, thus hinting at the underworld character of Moran's journey. Shortly thereafter, he encounters a pilgrim whom John Fletcher identifies with "C," one of the two men Molloy had seen early in his quest. However, it seems more likely that the man Moran encounters is Molloy himself; he wears a huge greatcoat and a strange hat, like Molloy, has a shock of long white hair, and has Molloy's characteristic diffident, gentle manner. Whoever he is, the man asks for bread and Moran offers him fish. The passage is a reference either to Matthew 7:9, "Or what man is there of you, whom if his son ask bread, will he give him a stone?" or Matthew 15:36, "And he took the seven loaves and the fishes . . . and gave to his disciples. . . ." Moran also gives the stranger the last piece of bread, which he had been saving for his son. The stranger breaks the bread and puts it in his pocket. He is turning to leave when Moran asks to see the walking stick; he finds it strangely light in spite of its heavy appearance and returns it to the stranger who walks away. The stick may have some association with Moses' rod, which symbolizes the divine power, or with the Cross itself. It is noteworthy that Moran stares at the other pilgrim for a long time and then himself cuts a stick. While waiting in the woods for his son, cut off from material possessions and distractions, Moran feels himself changing inwardly: "And on myself too I pored, on me so changed from what I was. . . . And what I saw was more like

a crumbling, a frenzied collapsing of all that had always protected me from all I was condemned to be. Or it was like a kind
of clawing *towards a light and countenance I could not name,* [italics
mine] that I had once known and long denied" (203), ". . . a
further index of the great changes I had suffered and of my
growing resignation to being dispossessed of self" (204).

On the second day, as he is stripping a branch of a tree, he is
struck by pity for the tree. One would be inclined to pass this
over as simply a natural reaction, for Moran does appear to
love nature, if not man. However, he speaks of the dragon-tree
of Teneriffe, by which Beckett draws attention to the symbolism of the tree with the snake wrapped around it, sometimes
seen in the form of a caduceus. This tree obviously is a symbol
of the Tree in the Garden of Eden. At the moment that he
contemplates this tree, which incidentally will not burn, a man
comes up suddenly behind him, a man who resembles himself.
Moran becomes enraged, apparently blacks out, and when he
returns to consciousness he finds the man dead. Is this murder
a real crime, that is, murder of a brother (Cain), or a fellow-
human (Judas)? Or is it murder of himself, the killing of the
Old Man so that the New one can emerge? In view of the
associations of the tree with the Fall and the fact that he is in
effect in an inferno, I am inclined to believe it is the latter. This
impression is justified by the fact that when his son returns and
looks at his father curiously, Moran cries, "I had a fall . . . did
you never have a fall?" (213). He immediately thinks then of
the mandrake (man plus dragon [snake]), which traditionally
springs from the seed of an executed murderer. Pages 214–
215 are replete with references to wrath and rage, others of the
deadly sins. Finally, they mount the bicycle and, riding off together, come to Ballyba, the town presumably where they expect to find Molloy. On the way they, too, pass a shepherd.
Beckett's description is simple, accurate, and breathtaking:

> The shepherd watched me as I came, without getting up.
> The dog too, without barking. The sheep too. Yes, little by
> little, one by one, they turned and faced me, watching me
> as I came. Here and there faint movements of recoil, a tiny
> foot stamping the ground, betrayed their uneasiness. They
> did not seem timid, as sheep go. And my son of course

watched me as I went, I felt his eyes in my back. The silence was absolute. Profound in any case. All things considered it was a solemn moment. The weather was divine. It was the close of day. Each time I stopped I looked about me. I looked at the shepherd, the sheep, the dog and even at the sky. . . . I gave thanks for evening that brings out the lights, the stars in the sky and on earth the brave little lights of men. By day the shepherd would have raised his pipe . . . And so in perfect order, the shepherd silent and the dog unneeded, the little flock departed. And so no doubt they would plod on, until they came to the stable or the fold. And there the shepherd stands aside to let them pass and he counts them as they go by, though he knows not one is missing. (217–219)

Again we see the characteristic features of a mystical state or vision: silence, gleaming lights, a sense of unity, or at least yearning for it. The vision ends when "a kind of immense sigh all around me announced it was not I who was departing but the flock" (220).

But though he would like to follow the shepherd, he does not, and instead he has a violent scene with his son, who disappears in the night. Moran is now alone, "powerless to act, or perhaps strong enough at last to act no more" (221). (Note the resemblance to Molloy's passivity: "Molloy could stay where he happened to be.") But he is reduced to very bad straits, feeling frightened and powerless, hoping that Molloy will find him "and grow to be a friend and like a father, . . . so that Youdi would not be angry" (222). He refers to one Obidil, whom, using St. Paul's phraseology, he longs to see "face to face." Cohn interprets "Obidil" as "Libido," but this seems inconsistent with the rest of Beckett's terminology and reference points, which are classical Christian rather then Freudian. The phrase from St. Paul ("See God face to face") would indicate that Obidil is the Deity. For what it is worth, according to *The Interpreter's Dictionary of the Bible,* Obed was the son of Boaz and Ruth, the grandfather of David, and therefore an ancestor of Jesus. The same source indicates that "El" (-il) is a Semitic name for the Deity. In addition, the Index-Lexicon to the Old Testament in Young's *Concordance to the Bible* indicates that "obed" is the past participle of the verb "abad," which means serving or being a servant. Thus "Obidil" is the servant of the Lord but also the Deity Himself, none other than Christ himself, in fact.

As time passes, Moran grows weaker "and more and more content . . . content with myself, almost elated . . ." (223). Then Gaber suddenly arrives and orders him home. Querying Gaber about Youdi, he is told that the latter says, "Life is a thing of beauty . . . and a joy for ever" (226). Most critics see this only as irony, which it undoubtedly is, but then the mystic's whole approach to life is paradoxical (and thus related to irony). For the mystic, in the midst of untold misery life is still a thing of beauty because it permits the possibility of approach to Absolute Being.

Moran has been "all winter on the way" (227), and when he returns home it is spring—obvious symbolism for death and resurrection of the spirit. Not that he is completely changed; far from it. He is still preoccupied with nit-picking theological questions and questions about his private life (228–231). Critics have fixed on question fourteen: "Might not the beatific vision become a source of boredom in the long run?" (229) as evidence that Beckett is laughing at the whole concept of divine perfection. But Rudolph Otto, in *The Idea of the Holy*, points out that to the natural man (which Moran certainly still is), the beatific vision must inevitably seem tedious, boring, or uninteresting, because he does not understand it. *Das Heilige* appeared in German first in 1917, was published in English translation in 1923, and has been frequently reprinted since. Thus it could conceivably have been read by Beckett, who spent some time in Germany during his wandering before settling in Paris. Many of its insights and incidental comments bear a remarkable resemblance to ideas implied or expressed ironically by Beckett. Interestingly enough, Otto is the only theologian or religious writer I consulted who mentioned Geulincx.

A trivial point which perhaps confirms Fletcher's (and my own) conviction that Youdi represents God occurs in question thirteen: "Was Youdi's business address still 8, Acacia Square?" (230). According to George Ferguson's *Signs and Symbols in Christian Art*, the acacia is a symbol of immortality and "eight" is the number of the Resurrection. If the explication seems absurd, it cannot be helped; Beckett probably laughed when he wrote it. Writing religious allegory does not, it seems, deprive one of a sense of humor.

Moran backslides as he contemplates the dance of his beloved bees; he falls again into the logical ratiocination which Beckett reserves for especial contempt and which blocks the mystical consciousness of unity. Moran has analyzed the dance of the bees and classified their figures and rhythms. He is attached to this analysis, naturally, not only because he does genuinely love the bees, but because the analysis is an assertion of his individual ego, a "glass-bead game," which promises infinite rewards to subtle pride. The passage about the bees ends with the comment: "And I would never do my bees the wrong I had done my God, to whom I had been taught to ascribe my angers, fears, desires, and even my body" (233). This is an attack in passing on the anthropomorphization of God, which is the most marked feature of all popular religion, and one which Beckett regards with particular disdain, as is amply evident in *Waiting for Godot*.

On his long pilgrimage home, in all kinds of inclement weather, suffering from cold, damp, dirt, and weariness, Moran encounters a farmer who roughly questions why Moran is on his land. He gives a lying answer, that he is making a pilgrimage to the Turdy Madonna, who saved his wife's life in childbirth. "This incident gives but a feeble idea of my ability," he says ironically, "even at this late period" (238). It is perhaps only coincidence that in Canto XXXI, lines 7–9, of the *Paradiso*, Dante uses the figure of a swarm of bees and that later in the same canto, he sees the vision of St. Mary. If we are to take this coincidence seriously, obviously Moran's bees and his turdy madonna indicate irony, but at Moran's expense, not at the expense of St. Mary.

When he gets home, he finds the house and garden deserted; the bees have died and dried into a little light ball. Every phrase expresses Moran's detachment from his whole previous life. He receives a visit from the priest, who talks to him. "He was right," says Moran, but immediately follows that comment with the detached, "Who is not right?" (240). He receives a visit from Gaber, who wants the report. "That's funny," thinks Moran, "I thought I was done with people and talk" (240). He sells all he has, following Christ's injunction to the rich young ruler. He goes into his garden and this section ends, as Molloy's did, with an evocation of the birds, the symbols of the divine spirit:

> My birds had not been killed. They were wild birds. And yet quite trusting. I recognized them and they seemed to recognize me. But one never knows. Some were missing and some were new. I tried to understand their language better. Without having recourse to mine. They were the longest, loveliest days of all the year. I lived in the garden. I have spoken of a voice telling me things. I was getting to know it better now, to understand what it wanted. It did not use the words that Moran had been taught when he was little and that he in his turn had taught to his little one. So that at first I did not know what it wanted. But in the end I understood this language. I understood it, I understood it, all wrong perhaps. That is not what matters. It told me to write the report. Does this mean I am freer now than I was? I do not know. I shall learn. Then I went back into the house and wrote, It is midnight. The rain is beating on the windows. It was not midnight. It was not raining. (240)

Thus the first novel in the trilogy ends with theophany. A start has been made on the negative way, but the *personae* are not very far advanced along the road and are in some doubt and ignorance. Even so, they will not abandon it.

IV

The Soul in its Cage:
The Quest of MacMann

It is a terrible thing to feel all that one possesses slipping away.

Pascal

The very title of *Malone Dies* indicates a further descent of the M–character or man into the Dark Night of the soul. Malone's encumbrances are reduced even more than those of Molloy and Moran but he is on the same quest, the religious quest which involves stripping away of possessions and eventually experiencing a mystical communion. Malone lives in a single room, in a bed, with only a few last possessions to which, however, he still clings passionately. He dreads to lose his stick with which he brings to himself the two pots necessary for his existence. He must eat, he must eliminate, he still has sexuality, of a sort. And above all, he clings to his pad and pencil, to his function as artist, as creator. Here is the Promethean, the Daedalian ego, which he *cannot* surrender. Possibly Beckett has in mind his friend Joyce's *A Portrait of the Artist,* in which the artist risks damnation in a theological sense rather than forego his vocation. But the opposition is not between pursuing one's artistic vocation in freedom or serving the church and one's country, as the immature Stephen thought; Beckett's relentless intellect pushes the conflict to the ultimate, the conflict between one's own ego and surrender to the all-encompassing divine.

Harvey, Cohn, and other critics have paid a good deal of attention to the Saposcats, the Lamberts, and the other creatures of Malone, the writer. But with the exception of Mac-

Mann and Lemuel, the other characters are quite unimportant, as Beckett is making clear through the absurdity and triviality of the stories in which they figure. Actually, the Saposcat-Lambert story seems to be a parody of rural novels of earth and lust like those by Thomas Hardy and Mary Webb. As Malone says, it is a tedious tale. The one really important story is that of Malone (and of all the other creatures beginning with "M," i.e., Man), whose only true religious vocation lies in the timeless moments when he yields his self-centered self. Over and over, the ambivalent yearning to lose oneself, one's ego, is expressed and re-expressed:

> What I sought, when I struggled out of my hole, then aloft through the stinging air towards an inaccessible boon, was the rapture of vertigo, the letting go, the fall, the gulf, the relapse to darkness, to nothingness. . . .(19)

> And if I close my eyes, close them really, as others cannot, but as I can, for there are limits to my impotence, then sometimes my bed is caught up into the air and tossed like a straw by the swirling eddies, and I in it. Fortunately it is not so much an affair of eyelids, but as it were the soul that must be veiled, that soul denied in vain, vigilant, anxious, turning in its cage as in a lantern, in the night without haven or craft or matter or understanding. (47–48)

> And during all this time, so fertile in incidents and mishaps, in my head I suppose all was streaming and emptying away as through a sluice, to my great joy, until finally nothing remained, either of Malone or of the other. And what is more I was able to follow without difficulty the various phases of this deliverance. . . . (50)

> Did I say I only say a small proportion of the things that come into my head? I must have. I choose those that seem somehow akin. It is not always easy. I hope they are the most important. I wonder if I shall ever be able to stop. Perhaps I should throw away my lead. I could never retrieve it now. I might be sorry. My little lead. It is a risk I do not feel inclined to take, just now. (81–82)

Such passages are interspersed with parts of the Saposcat-Lambert-MacMann story, with bits of personal narration, and with sardonic comments on the functions of the body and the futility of existence.

The opening of *Malone Dies* appears to be about the act of dying. In my view, this may be actual physical dying, but is certainly dying to the world—the process of detachment in the face of the last things. The date is given, somewhat cagily, as March or April ("Perhaps next month [he will die]. Then it will be the month of April or of May." [1]). Beckett's allowing for *either* March *or* April must be a covert reference to the movable dates of Good Friday and Easter, hinting at the questions of judgment and salvation. A number of phrases suggest the attempt to reach the mystic's state of detachment and tranquillity: "I will not weigh upon the balance any more, one way or the other. I shall be neutral and inert. . . . I shall pay less heed to myself. . . . I shall not watch myself die, that would spoil everything" (1–2).

Malone says, "While waiting, I shall tell myself stories, if I can" (2). This waiting is waiting for death but is also at the same time the waiting upon God of the classical mystical technique. He makes it clear that he no longer has an egotistical object in telling these stories; it is now merely a game (as in Zen) to while away the time. Yet he cannot maintain the detached stance: "It does not matter if I do not finish. But if I finish too soon? That does not matter either," he tells himself (3). He fusses about leaving an inventory of his possessions, then reminds himself that nothing of all this matters any more ("There I am back at my old quibbles" [4]). Against his better judgment because of the ego-involvement, he describes his present state, stressing that he is living in an ordinary room in an ordinary house, contrary to all those critics who insist that Beckett's characters inhabit mental hospitals or asylums. He is not clear as to how he came there; he simply accepts his habitation, noting that simple explanations are the best, even when they do not explain very much: "A bright light is not necessary, a taper is all one needs to live in strangeness if it faithfully burns" (5). Pascal expresses an almost similar thought in *Pensée* 483: "There is enough light for those whose only desire is to see, and enough darkness for those of a contrary disposition." Malone vaguely remembers a forest, and says that "perhaps" he was stunned by a blow. It is less important whether this vague memory indicates he is Molloy or Moran, than to note the forest (place of error and confusion, as in Dante), and that he stresses "all that belongs to the past" (6), indicating a change of direction or values. There is a window in his room through which he watches the stars (again reminding us of Dante), the moon, and the birds, here as in *Molloy* and in all literature a symbol of the divine. He is looked after by an unseen agency, whose deputy is a good old woman, whom he does not describe physically, thus reminding us of the shadowy Sophie in Molloy's book. Since women in the trilogy are usually hideous hags of unnatural concupiscence, it is noteworthy that the three who are more or less beneficent (one in each book) are not evoked carnally. "She is an old woman. I don't know why she is good to me. Yes, let us call it goodness, without quibbling. For her it is certainly goodness. I believe her to be even older than I. . . . All I see of her now is the gaunt hand and part of the sleeve. Not even that, not even that" (8).

Somewhere in the turmoil of his body, Malone says, "Thought struggles on, it too wide of the mark" (9), probably an allusion to Philippians 3:14: "I press toward the mark for the prize of the high calling of God." Also, of course, to miss the mark is the original meaning of the Greek word *hamartanein* meaning "to sin." In the words of Alan Watts, "the mark or point here— equivalent to the 'strait and narrow gate' or the 'needle's eye' which is the entrance to heaven—is the timeless eternal moment wherein our real life counts. To be 'off the mark' is to be identi- fied with the past . . ." (99). The Saposcat narrative is inter- rupted by anxious personal statements. Malone is concerned because he has not been able to play, to invent, in a detached manner. He seeks "him waiting for me always, who needed me and whom I needed, who took me in his arms and told me to stay with him always, who gave me his place and watched over me, who suffered every time I left him, whom I have often made suffer and seldom contented, whom I have never seen" (19). This passage has an apposite parallel in Pascal's *Pensée* 699: "True conversion consists in self-annihilation before the Univer- sal Being whom we have so often provoked and who has reason to destroy us every hour. . . ." But Malone is afflicted with nag- ging egotistical anxieties: "What fine things, what momentous things, I am going to miss through fear, fear of falling back into the old error, fear of not finishing in time, fear of revelling for the first time, in a last outpouring of misery, impotence and hate. The forms are many in which the unchanging seeks relief from its formlessness" (21). The last striking phrase possibly owes something to Plotinus, to Augustine, or to Meister Eckhart. Speaking of God, Plotinus says: "For even while it [the mind of God] is active, it contemplates. When it produces it produces forms" (Happold, 187). In the twelfth book of *The Confessions* St. Augustine, speaking of chaos, says that "all this whole was almost nothing, because hitherto it was altogether without form; but yet there was now something about to be formed. For Thou, Lord, madest the world of a matter without form." Eckhart says in Tractate XI: "God is his own form and matter; his form emerges from his matter and according to this form does he form all things that become" (Happold, 240).

Very soon after, in "such a night as Kasper David Friedrich loved"[17] (22), Malone appears to have a mystical experience of the same partial order as those of Molloy:

> Now that I have looked I hear the wind. I close my eyes and it mingles with my breath. Words and images run riot in my head, pursuing, flying, clashing, merging, endlessly. But beyond this tumult there is a great calm, and a great indifference, never really to be troubled by anything again.

It might be contended that this passage vindicates Barnard and other critics who see the passage as a return-to-the-womb fantasy. Given that he next reminisces about his childhood, perhaps it is a fetal fantasy. And yet—some of the same signs are presented in the other "visions": the wind (mentioned twice), calmness and indifference, his head is turned "like a bird's" (23).

[17]Kasper David Friedrich, German painter, 1774–1840. According to Marcel Brion in *Romantic Art*, "Friedrich belongs to the German Romantic school of painting, and expresses a 'mystical conception of nature . . . in a manner not unlike that of Blake.' " Among the color plates included in Brion's volume is a striking painting of "The Cross and the Cathedral" (Plate No. XXXI, p. 112), presently in the Kunts-museum in Dusseldorf. Another, at the National Gallery in Berlin, is called "Man and Woman Gazing at the Moon" (Plate XXXII, p. 114). Both these pictures emanate a mysterious, brooding, almost mythic quality very appropriate to Beckett's own "landscapes."

... Can it be Easter Week? Thus with the year Seasons return. If it can, could not this song I have just heard, and which quite frankly is not yet quite stilled within me, could not this song have simply been to the honour and glory of him who was the first to rise from the dead, to him who saved me, twenty centuries in advance? Did I say the first? The final bawl lends colour to this view. (33)

In spite of the seeming mockery at the end, the passage expresses some nostalgia. The song is "not yet quite stilled within me" (33). One should note, too, that Easter is a climactic moment in the quests of both Langland and Dante, and also in the personal quest of Simone Weil (68)—more climactic certainly than it is here, where it is only a memory.

A little later, Malone comments that he does not "depart from [himself] now with the same avidity as a week ago for example" (33). He repeats this twice; thus we are entitled to consider it important. It is a recognized phenomenon among mystics that the grace of partial or complete union comes quite at random, sometimes frequently, other times at long intervals or not at all, and it seems that Malone's comment might appertain to this randomness of the mystical experience.

After another long chunk of tedious narration about the Lamberts, Malone remembers an "Israelite" friend of his named Jackson. A whole series of "whoresons" whose names all end in "-son" found Malone disgusting, nor was he any more successful among persons of other races, or with the sick and insane. Malone speculates about the house where he lives, full of babies and parents, and quotes Lucretius: "Suave mari Magno" (44)—"It is sweet to stand above the turbulent seas." He wonders if he died in the forest, but concludes he did not. He discusses the nature of the light (45–46) just as Molloy did; it is neither dark nor bright, but a grayish light, as it was for Molloy. This midlight seems to correspond not only to the modern Purgatorial world, but to the first dark night of St. John of the Cross, the night of the senses. According to F. C. Happold, speaking of St. John of the Cross in *Mysticism:* "In the first night there is, he says, some light, for understanding and reason still operate" (60).

Pages 48–52 in *Malone Dies* record a true mystical experience, "of which nothing will ever be known," although at the same time it happened, Malone was reaching for his pencil. It begins: " . . . they brought me the solution and conclusion of the whole sorry business of Malone (since that is what I am called now) and of the other, for the rest is no business of mine. And it was, though more unutterable, like the crumbling away of two little heaps of fine sand, or dust, or ashes of unequal size, but diminishing together as it were in ratio, if that means anything, and leaving behind them, each in its own stead, the blessedness of absence" (48). It culminates with the beautiful description of the hand "plunged in me up to the elbow":

> And I must say that to me at least and for as long as I can remember the sensation is familiar of a blind and tired hand delving feebly in my particles and letting them trickle between its fingers. And sometimes, when all is quiet, I feel it plunged in me up to the elbow, but gently, and as though sleeping. But soon it stirs, wakes, fondles, clutches, ransacks, ravages, avenging its failure to scatter me with one sweep. (50–51)

This description is analogous to Exodus 33:121–23: "And the Lord said . . . I will put thee in a cleft of the rock, and will cover thee with my hand, while I pass by; and I will take away my hand, and thou shalt see my back parts; but my face shall not be seen." One might question the use of "blind" and "tired" for the divine hand, and what is the "failure to scatter me with one sweep"? Yet indubitably a sense that one is in the hand of someone or something has all kinds of traditional connotations. Hitchcock's *Cruden's Concordance* shows thirty-two entries under "Hand of the Lord," and several others applying to the divine under "My Hand" or "Hand." The great majority of these references are in the prophetic books of the Bible, for example, Jeremiah 21:4–6 and Amos 9:2. Probably the above passage is a description of failed attempts at mystic communion, in which, however, the initiative is ascribed to the divine, and therefore the failure—ironically.

As a relief from his memories, he makes himself another creature. Malone names him MacMann, which with ridiculous ease translates to "Son of Man," a phrase used by the Old Testament prophets to indicate the Chosen One, and the name by which Christ called himself. Use of this phrase hints again at

Beckett's view of Christ as being a paradigm of all suffering humanity. Malone describes the erotic encounters in the city at the end of the day (56–57) in a passage which is also reminiscent of *The Waste Land* (ll. 207–248). Like all the M-characters, MacMann is a homeless wanderer, and Malone speculates that perhaps he (MacMann) "has come to that stage of his instant when to live is to wander the last of the living in the depths of an instant without bounds" (59). The "instant without bounds" is very like the Boethian definition of eternity: "the whole, perfect and simultaneous possession of endless life" (*The Consolation of Philosophy*, Book V), and it also recalls Eliot's "moment in and out of time" (*Four Quartets, Dry Salvages,* V).

Malone interrupts MacMann's story to discuss his own increasing detachment from his body (61–62). Farther on, when Malone describes the "hole in the wall" through which he glimpses "extraordinary things" (64), one is reminded of St. Gregory's "chink of contemplation": "He who keeps his heart within, he it is who receives the light of contemplation. For they that still think immoderately of external things, know not what are the chinks of contemplation from the eternal light" (Butler, 72). But what Malone actually sees through his window has nothing to do with the eternal light—or does it? He describes, as a child might describe it, with a kind of wondering detachment, the lovemaking of a couple standing up by their window, and then turns quickly away from the scene back to MacMann.

MacMann lies down in the rain in the attitude of crucifixion as Molloy had done—again identifying both Molloy and MacMann as Christ figures. Malone says "And there comes the hour when nothing more can happen and nobody can come and all is ended but the waiting that knows itself in vain. Perhaps he had come to that" (68), which is a description of the passive "waiting on God," the contemplative discipline of the mystic. One would need to be waiting on God to lie out in the rain without protest, irritation, or definitive action. While MacMann lies there, Malone describes him in terms which emphasize his poverty and humility (71). But in the end, of course, MacMann (or Malone?) is unable to sustain his passivity, and Malone cries, "Quick, quick my possessions" (74). We are back in the familiar world of the clutching ego. As Pascal says (*Pensée* 350): "It is a terrible thing to feel all that one possesses slipping away."

Then Malone loses his stick, a very serious event for him in his moribund condition. In a bout of discouragement, he falls asleep and wakes to chide himself: "For why be discouraged, one of the thieves was saved. That is a generous precentage" (83), almost exactly what Vladimir says in *Waiting for Godot*. He returns for relief again to the story of MacMann. MacMann wakes up in the House of St. John of God—a suggestive name indeed with its echo of St. John of the Cross. Here he goes once again through the business of being stripped of clothes and possessions which is such an obsessive feature of Beckett's parables. Everything of his has been thrown away with the exception of the silver knife-rest, which he is told can be returned to him at any time (but it is not, or at least its return is not mentioned). The knife-rest is, of course, the little sawhorse with the two crosses stolen from Sophie Loy by Molloy. The importance of the knife-rest is not that it is a further link between Malone and Molloy but that it evokes the whole constellation of thoughts—judgment, suffering, redemption, salvation—associated with the two thieves. The fact that it has been prepared for by Malone's seemingly random reference to the thieves "lends colour to this view," to use Beckett's own words (33).

There follows what in a medieval allegory such as *Piers the Ploughman,* for example, would be an episode illustrating Lust. MacMann is attended by one Moll, a figure as decrepit and disgusting as himself, and their efforts at intercourse are as repulsive as those between Molloy and his Ruth-Edith in the first book of the trilogy. This anecdote does have a kind of grim humor. Moll's letter to her beloved is especially funny, if one can be amused by this kind of irony. It is harder to see the function of such a gross relationship within either MacMann's story or Malone's than it was to understand it in the story of Molloy, where it emerged as a memory of past sexuality. It seems reasonable to suppose that the affair with Moll is the second of three expressions of concupiscence (one in each book). That this is the likely explanation is strengthened by the fact that in the preamble to this material, Malone reports "extraordinary heat . . . which has seized on certain parts of my economy" (88). And, of course, earlier he had witnessed through his window an act of sexual intercourse, although he had seemed detached enough at time of viewing.

For many persons the most grisly part of the Moll-MacMann affair is the crucifixion scene portrayed by Moll's lone tooth and her two earrings. Many critics, notably Ruby Cohn, see this as an attack on the church and Christianity. Although this might have been likely in Beckett's younger days, when he wrote *Whoroscope* and *More Pricks than Kicks*, it is unlikely that in this, his mature work, he is indulging himself in such cheap gibes. For one thing, Moll as the church does not parallel Ruth-Edith, who does not appear to represent anything except concupiscence. And parallels are as important to Beckett's style as they are to Dante's, as we shall see later. For another, Moll's tooth and earrings reintroduce the theme of the two thieves and Christ's passion and death, which haunt the entire trilogy. The episode is, as usual, part of Beckett's Manichean attack on sexuality, but it has been manipulated to highlight the theme of salvation.

Lemuel, who comes and tells MacMann that Moll is dead, is moody, forgetful, sometimes very good-humored, sometimes appearing insane. Although one first tends to associate the name Lemuel with Lemuel Gulliver, the name itself means "devoted to God," or "belonging to God." One might assume its use here to be ironic, if it were not for the fact that in the end Lemuel kills the guardians and takes MacMann out to sea (usually a symbol of the divine). Lemuel, then, is another "messenger," like Gaber. Fletcher is mistaken in saying that Lemuel is brutal and beats MacMann for tearing up the hyacinth. Careful reading shows that the narrator (Malone) changes Lemuel's action in mid-sentence: "Then Lemuel took it from him and struck him with it over and over again, no that won't work, then Lemuel called a keeper by the name of Pat. . . . Then Pat snatched the stick from MacMann . . . and struck him with it until Lemuel told him to stop. . . . " When MacMann tears up the hyacinth, he is "fiercely reprimanded by Lemuel who wrenched the pretty flower from his hands and threatened to hand him over . . . to Pat again. . . ." The moderating influence of Lemuel is clear evidence that the story of MacMann is important to Malone in a way that the Lambert-Saposcat story is not.

Malone has a visit from a strange person who looks like an undertaker, who, after giving him a blow on his head to attract his attention, leaves without saying anything. Malone himself is too surprised to communicate with him, although he longs to. The need for human companionship reasserts itself for a few pages (102–104). Then Malone returns to the story of Mac-Mann. Followed by his keepers, MacMann roams in the park of the House of St. John, and pulls up a hyacinth by the roots. Although the hyacinth is not the same flower which the Greeks knew by that name, it was supposed to have sprung from the blood of the slain vegetation god, Hyacinthus, and its petals to have formed the Greek syllables for a cry of mourning, "AI AI." Although Lemuel had kept the others from beating Mac-Mann for destroying a laurel bush (symbol of wordly accomplishment), he now—seemingly inconsistently—snatches the hyacinth from MacMann's hand and reprimands him. But the hyacinth is in a special category, one that is obvious enough to the reader of Eliot's *The Waste Land* and Frazer's *The Golden Bough*. The hyacinth incident carries forward the theme of the crucifixion and the resurrection which is so much the "still center" of this "novel." Now the discussion of the action shades imperceptibly into Malone's own feelings. It has been obvious for some time that Malone's preoccupation with the last things is intruding upon the narrative. Preceded by the inevitable passage about the wheeling and crying birds which so often introduces the metaphysical flights, he cries that all these —Sapo, Moll, and presumably also MacMann and Lemuel though he does not mention them—are a "pretext for not coming to the point, the abandoning, the raising of the arms and going down, without further splash, even though it may annoy the bathers" (107). Although he is literally describing a drowning, it is "the awful daring of a moment's surrender," to use Eliot's phrase. The text continues:

> Yes, there is no good pretending, it is hard to leave everything. The horror-worn eyes linger abject on all they have beseeched so long, in a last prayer, *the true prayer at last, the one that asks for nothing* [italics mine]. And it is then a little breath of fulfillment revives the dead longings and a murmur is born in the silent world, reproaching you affectionately with having despaired too late. The last word in the way of viaticum. Let us try it another way. The pure plateau. (107)

"The prayer that asks for nothing" sounds as though it is in the classic religious tradition, but the sense of the passage following indicates that it really *is* a prayer for nothing, a prayer of despair. But *at the same moment* comes "the little breath of fulfillment . . . a murmur . . . reproaching you affectionately. . . ." The little murmur is a viaticum (or Eucharist given to the dying).

But Malone turns away from the little murmur and turns back to description of the House of St. John of God, which stands on a mount, like Dante's purgatory, "called the Rock," significantly or ironically capitalized. (Matt. 16:18: "and upon this rock will I build my church." Cf. also Eliot's *Choruses from "The Rock,"* and the Book of Psalms, especially 61:2 and 62:5–6.) MacMann, too, like the narrator, is trying to accept the negative situation, the negation of all ordinary desires and feelings:

> seeking a way out into the desolation of having nobody and nothing, the wilds of the hunted, the scant bread and the scant shelter and the black joy of the solitary way, in helplessness and will-lessness, through all the beauty, the knowing and the loving. (108–109)

It can be argued that both Malone and McMann are contemplating physical death in such passages, but there is no evidence that either is going to commit suicide, and in any case one has to account for such phrases as "the beauty, the knowing and the loving." The story ends, significantly, on an Easter weekend, with an absurd and pathetic scene: several inmates of the House of St. John of God, along with an idiot female aristocrat bent on giving them a treat, go on a boating excursion, accompanied by Lemuel, who kills the two guards and puts out to sea with MacMann and the patients. Here the narrative is interrupted, as Malone has a vision of light:

> The night is strewn with absurd lights, stars, the beacons, the buoys, the lights of earth and in the hills the faint fires of the blazing gorse. (119)

Book One had ended with birds (twice); this second book ends with a vision of light which while perhaps not a beatific vision, is at least a glimpse of the divine as the narrator's voice trails away.

V

The Black Void:
The Quest of Mahood

A shade uncast, a light unshed

Samuel Beckett

In *The Unnamable* the religious allegory persists, but we are done with masks and *personae*. The *persona* is quite candidly the narrator, called incorrectly by most critics the "Unnamable." The term "the unnamable" has been used since antiquity to refer to God, who as creator of the world is analogous to the creator of the world of this and other Beckettian novels. In Jewish doctrine the name of God must never be uttered, and He is given another name, Adonai, by which He may be spoken of outside the sanctuary of the synagogue. Additionally, many of the mystics refer to God as the Unnamable One; for example, Ruysbroeck, in *The Seven Degrees of Love* says: "There the Godhead is, in simple essence, without activity; Eternal Rest, Unconditioned Dark, the Nameless Being, the Superessence of all created things," (Happold, 66). Nicholas of Cusa in *Of Learned Ignorance* says: "*Thou* mayest not be attained, comprehended, or named, or multiplied, or beheld" (Happold, 308). Thus since the term "Unnamable" stands for the Creator, the unnamable in this story must be Beckett himself. The terms of the metaphoric equation are: Worm and Mahood are to the narrator as the narrator is to Beckett, as Beckett is to God. But if the narrator is created in the image of Beckett, then we are entitled to regard whatever is true of the narrator as being true of Beckett—or are we? Is what is true of man true also of God?

Alan Watts offers an interesting speculation on the nature of God as artist-creator, which seems pertinent here.

> God gives *himself* to creatures, so that free will is not the property of any creature in so far as he is an individual, but only in so far as the actual reality of his being, his true Self, *is* God and acts as God. To the extent, then, that creatures act freely they are performing what are essentially the actions of God. God himself is therefore the true actor, playing the many parts of the world-drama. But the drama is "play," not "reality," and "art" or "seeming" rather than "truth." (33)

Watts' metaphysics are very likely based on those of Nicholas of Cusa:

> And creating and being created alike are naught else than the sharing of Thy Being among all, that Thou mayest be All in all, and yet mayest abide freed from all. For to call into being things which are not is to make Nothing a sharer in Being: thus to call is to create, while to share is to be created. And beyond this coincidence of creating and being created art Thou, Absolute and Infinite God, neither creating nor creatable, albeit all things are what they are because Thou art. (Happold, 307)

To one looking at the trilogy as a metaphoric projection of the mystic way, the whole first page of the third novel is redolent with mystical terminology: ". . . one day I simply stayed in, in where, instead of going out, in the old way. . . . Perhaps I simply assented at last to an old thing. But I did nothing. I shall have to speak of things of which I cannot speak" (3). (Cf. Meister Eckhart: "Why dost thou prate of God? Whatever thou sayest of Him is untrue" [Happold, 64], or Jung: "Every statement about the transcendental ought to be avoided because it is a laughable presumption on the part of the human mind, unconscious of its limitations" [Happold, 64].)

The narrator admits that he is haunted by the creatures of his imagination, although he hopes eventually to be rid of them. He appears to be in a dim, dark place with intermittent lights. This is undoubtedly the second Dark Night of the Soul. Returning to Eliot, we find a similar ambiance in *Burnt Norton*, III:

Descend lower, descend only
Into the world, of *perpetual solitude,*
World not world, but that which is not world.
Internal darkness, *deprivation*
And destitution of all property,
Desiccation of the world of sense,
Evacuation of the world of fancy,

[italics mine]

In the dark world of *The Unnamable,* the narrator is immobilized, without property or any recognizable realistic accouterments. Even the hat and the little knife-rest are now gone. On page 8, he talks about being (he thinks) at the center rather than on the circumference, an allusion to the definition of God as one whose circumference is nowhere and whose center is everywhere. Ascribed to Augustine by the *Oxford Dictionary of the Christian Church,* this definition is ascribed to St. Bonaventure by Alan Watts in *Myth and Ritual in Christianity,* and to *The Book of the Twenty-Four Philosophers* by Joseph Campbell in *Myths to Live By.* According to David Hesla, it is also found in Pascal, Meister Eckhart, and Nicholas of Cusa (14), the latter two being important Christian mystics. It must be a very old definition, of intense symbolical significance. The narrator's allusion may also owe something to St. John of the Cross, who speaks of "the centre" in *The Living Flame of Love:* "The centre of the soul is God; and, when the soul has attained to Him according to the whole capacity of its being, . . . it will have reached the last and deep centre of the soul" (Happold, 331). The German mystic, Jacob Boehme, says: "Cease from thine own activity, fix thine eyes upon one point. . . . Gather in all thy thoughts and by faith press on to the centre" (Happold, 75). Simone Weil also speaks of God as the center: "He whose soul remains ever turned in the direction of God while the nail pierces it, finds himself nailed on to the very centre of the universe. It is the true centre, it is not in the middle, it is beyond space and time, it is God" (135). (Note also her preoccupation with the nails, hammer and cross, noticed by several critics about Beckett.) Again, the mention of the centre may be to draw attention to the analogy between the artist-creator and the Creator.

The narrator wonders how long he has been in this "place"

("state" would be a better word), and after vacillating, concludes that "this place was made for me and I for it, at the same
instant" (11), an equivocation that would indicate that he is "out
of time." The place also is silent, although paradoxically he can
hear occasional sounds.

The narrator talks about how he has only faked it in the "other
world," and about the empty instructions and education he received before he detached himself from the world. He refers to
his leading preceptor as "Basil." A bishop of the early church,
Basil was one who had had mystical experience, according to
Hans Lietzmann in *History of the Early Church* (197–198), and he
also laid down rules and disciplines for the ascetic life.

The narrator's voice spins on, even though he knows he
should empty his mind: "Method or no method I shall have to
banish them in the end, the beings, things, shapes, sounds and
lights with which my haste to speak has encumbered this place"
(15). But in vain does he pursue total detachment; his creatures
are more "god-like" in that sense than he (15). Another paradoxical expression of the analogy to the Creator is on page 18:
"I am Matthew and I am the angel, I who came before the
cross, before the sinning, came into the world, came here."
("Before Abraham was I AM," John 8:58.) He speaks of the
place where he is as "perhaps merely the inside of my distant
skull," reminding us once again of lines from Eliot's *Murder in
the Cathedral,* written long before Beckett's:

> It was here, in the kitchen, in the passage,
> In the mews in the barn in the byrne in the marketplace
> In our veins our bowels our skulls as well. . . .
> (*Complete Poems and Plays,* 208)

> Still the horror, but more horror
> Than when twisting in the fingers,
> Than when splitting in the skull.
> (210)

Surely it is a striking coincidence that Eliot's play then contemplates the void:

> The white flat face of Death, God's silent servant
> And behind the face of Death the Judgement

And behind the Judgement, the Void
more horrid than active shapes of hell;
Emptiness, absence, separation from God; . . .

And a few lines further on in *The Unnamable*, Beckett too, or
rather his surrogate, is speaking of the void: "Only I and this
black void have ever been" (21). Such coincidences may be and
probably are entirely unconscious and subliminal on Beckett's
part, yet to me they indicate similar preoccupations on the part
of Eliot and Beckett.

The narrator of *The Unnamable* has lost his sense organs and
is detached from all bodily functions (22–25), yet the irrepres-
sible ego remains: "I have no voice and must speak, with this
voice that is not mine, but can only be mine, since there is no
one but me, or if there are others, to whom it might belong. . . . So it is I who speak, all lone, since I can't do otherwise" (26). He decides to rename Basil Mahood (Manhood):
". . . his voice is there in mine, but less, less" (29), a comment
indicating that he is gradually weaning himself from the creative urge. Pages 31–32 are about the "pensum" he has to
perform before he can be free from his tyrants, "different in
their views as to what should be done with me, in conclave
since time began or a little later, listening to me from time to
time, then breaking up for a meal or a game of cards" (31).
This description of the tyrants idly eating or playing cards
evokes another religious allegory, Kafka's *The Hunger Artist,*
and his description of the butchers who watch the hunger
artist. The narrator's one hope is to perform the pensum so
that his mind may be "at peace, that is to say empty. . . .
Strange hope, turned towards silence and peace" (31). The
fact that it is an internal conflict, between the worldly and
unworldly elements in himself, is indicated by "the admission
that I am Mahood after all and these stories of a being whose
identity he usurps, and whose voice he prevents from being
heard, all lies from beginning to end" (32).

The rest of the book is a brilliant evocation of the spiritual
struggle between the creative ego of the writer, and the wish to
attain contemplative peace, the mystic union with the Absolute.
The narrator speaks of his master (obviously Beckett) in terms
which are analogous to those we use of God:

A little more explicitness on his part, since the initiative belongs to him, might be a help, as well from his point of view as from the one he attributes to me. Let the man explain himself and have done with it. It's none of my business to ask him questions, even if I knew how to reach him. Let him inform me once and for all what exactly it is he wants from me, for me. What he wants is my good, I know that, at least I say it, in the hope of bringing him around to a more reasonable frame of mind, assuming he exists and existing, hears me. But what good, there must be more than one. The supreme perhaps. In a word let him enlighten me, that's all I ask. . . . (34–35)

He pictures himself returning from a voyage across the world ("the vast and heaving wastes I had traversed" (41), to see a small rotunda in the midst of a yard full of dust and ashes (The Waste Land again? Gehenna?). His wife and family live in the rotunda. They comment on him rather disdainfully and treat him as a thing, rather than as a person. One of them says, "What about throwing him a sponge?" (42), an allusion to the bystander who offered Jesus a sponge filled with vinegar (Matt. 27:48). This entire episode reminds one of Matthew 10:35–36: "For I am come to set a man at variance against his father, and the daughter against her mother, and the daughter-in-law against her mother-in-law. And a man's foes shall be they of his own household." Again, the analogy works both ways. The creative artist is cut off from his family by his complete dedication to his work, just as the spiritual adept is cut off from those close to him by his dedication to the Absolute.

While he notices his family and their reactions, he remains somewhat detached from them: " . . . I had to husband my strength if I was ever to arrive. I had no wish to arrive, but I had to do my utmost, in order to arrive" (45). The use of the word "arrive," a rather odd one in the circumstances, since he is actually immobilized, echoes St. John of the Cross in the authoritative edition of Allison Peers (Happold, 330):

> In order to arrive at having pleasure in everthing
> Desire to have pleasure in nothing.
> In order to arrive at possessing everything
> Desire to possess nothing.

In order to arrive at being everything,
  Desire to be nothing.
In order to arrive at knowing everything,
  Desire to know nothing.

It is significant that that particular passage from St. John of the Cross is paraphrased by Eliot in the *Quartets*.

In spite of their comments upon the narrator, his family suddenly appear to have died of poisoning. At first he pretends to have turned away, sickened, then he recants and explains that he went into the rotunda and stamped upon the corpses. The episode of his rejection of and by his family rambles on for several pages and is written with same kind of brutality displayed by Beckett in describing the murders of the charcoal burner by Molloy and of the stranger who looked like himself by Moran, a brutality which is shocking but which perhaps is necessary to break through the reader's habitual conventionality and indifference. Beckett's extreme sensitivity to brutality is precisely the reason he evokes it so vividly; his pain (noted by his most perceptive critics, Fletcher and Harvey) reminds one of Simone Weil's comment in *Waiting for God:* " . . . still today when any human being . . . speaks to me without brutality, I cannot help having the impression that there must be a mistake and that unfortunately the mistake will in all probability disappear" (33).

Over and over the narrator speaks of "them," "their language," and how hard "they" tried to teach him to be one of them, to prevent him from doing what he had to do (51–53). In the end the egotistic creative image prevails; he says he will tell "another of Mahood's stories . . . to be understood . . . as being about me" (53). In this story, he is in a sealed jar up to his mouth; the jar is situated in a quiet street "near the shambles." The location near the shambles (where Molloy's mother lived) operates on two levels; from it he can see all the brutality of the world and of nature. Pascal's *Pensée* 341 is pertinent here: "let us imagine a number of men in chains and all condemned to death. Everyday some are butchered before the eyes of the rest and the survivors see their condition reflected in that of their fellows." Yet if my surmise is correct, the shambles is also an allusion to the Judeo-Christian tradition: sacrifice and redemption go hand in hand.

He is fed by the owner of a nearby chop-house, who also covers his head with a tarpaulin when it rains or snows. His neck is fixed in a collar, which, whether Beckett intends us to do so or not, makes me think of Herbert's metaphysical poem, "The Collar." (See also Herbert's "Miserie," in which the poet speaks of man as "a lump of flesh, without foot or wing"—an exact equivalent to the narrator's situation in the jar. Perhaps not coincidentally, Herbert's poem ends, "My God, I mean myself." It is interesting also that Pascal in *Pensée* 111 says, "I can imagine a man without hands, feet, or head. . . . But I cannot imagine a man without thought. . . .") The narrator meditates on how to outwit his tormentors so that he may cease "living," "so that they may be pleased with me, and perhaps leave me in peace at last, and free to do what I have to do, namely try and please *the other* [italics mine], if that is what I have to do, so that he may be pleased with me, and leave me in peace at last, and give me quittance, and the right to rest, and silence, if that is in his gift. . . . that peace where he neither is, nor is not, and where the language dies that permits of such expressions" (65–66). (Cf. "The peace of God which passeth all understanding," Phil. 4:7.) As I have already mentioned, in most modern works of theology God is referred to as "the other" or "the wholly other." For example, in *The Idea of the Holy* Otto speaks of "The downright stupendous-ness, the well-nigh daemonic and wholly incomprehensible character of the eternal creative power; how incalculable and 'wholly other,' it mocks at all conceiving" (80).

Pages 66–125 continue the description of how the narrator's preceptors drill him into being like themselves, creatures of this world. He now calls himself Worm, a lowlier form of life than Mahood (see Psalm 22: "I am a worm and no man," and also Herbert's "Sighs and Groans": "for thou only art the mightie God, but I am a sillie worm").[18] He realizes dimly that "Perhaps it's by trying to be Worm that I'll finally succeed in being Ma-

---

[18]Given Beckett's preoccupation with Good Friday, the day of the Crucifixion and also the day he claims as his birthday, the importance of Psalm 22 in his work cannot be overestimated, for it is used in the ancient office of Tenebrae on Good Friday. See Dierdre Bair, *Samuel Beckett: A Biography* (New York: Harcourt Brace Jovanovich, 1978), p. 4, for the problem of Beckett's birthdate.

hood" (72), in other words, that the fullness of humanity is achieved by recognizing the awfulness of "the other." He speaks of being hooked, and says, "The third line falls plumb from the skies, it's for her majesty, my soul" (72). This again echoes Herbert ("The Pearl": "But thy silk twist let down from heav'n to me"; "Prayer (I)": "The Christian plummet sounding heaven and earth"), but is undoubtedly an allusion to their common source in Amos 7:7–8: " . . . the Lord stood upon a wall made by a plumbline, with a plumbline in his hand. . . . Then said the Lord, 'Behold, I will set a plumbline in the midst of my people Israel. I will not again pass by them any more.' " (See also St. Catherine of Genoa, *The Dialogue:* ". . . with the finest golden thread. . . . I come down to man and to the thread a hook is fixed which catches his heart," O'Brien, 192.)

The words "affirmation" and "negation" hurtle past in the paradoxical monologue. He speaks of the sunset and of his shadow, which he used to contemplate before his head was fixed in the collar. The woman who covers his head is suddenly given the name Marguerite, the better perhaps to draw attention to the allusion to Faust a few lines further on. He sees "the sky . . . streaming into the main of the firmament" (75), a strange phrase that recalls Marlowe's Dr. Faustus. Evidently man's Faustian pride is still preventing him from attaining the peace of the transcendant. A little later, his caretaker's name is given as Madeline, a variant of Magdalene, the erstwhile prostitute who was one of the Marys around the cross of Christ. No question but the sealed jar is an analogue of the Crucifixion, particularly as Beckett describes all the indifferent passersby on their way to and from the shambles. As mentioned earlier, several critics have noted that Beckett has always associated the suffering Christ with suffering humanity, and this notion is strengthened by Christ's own use of the phrase "Son of Man" to describe himself. Beckett of course has drawn attention to the point by his use of "Mac-Mann" and Mahood" as titles for his surrogates. Although these same critics assume this to be a heretical point of view, there is a valid basis for it in orthodoxy. Both *The Gospel According to St. John* and Paul's *Epistle to the Romans* promise that mankind can become sons of God. "God was made man in order that man might be made God," said St. Athanasius (Happold, 63). And St. Maximus said: "A portion of the flesh and blood of each of us is in the man Christ" (Happold, 115). Both Langland and Dante imply that man shares in Christ's divinity—Langland through the symbolic figure of *Piers the Ploughman,* Dante through the enigmatic human figure at the center of the three circles of light in the beatific vision.[19] And in every Mass, both Catholic and Anglican, as the priest mixes the wine and water, he prays that men may share the divinity of Christ, as Christ shared our humanity.

He notes that although Madeline comes to see him more often than ever, she appears to be losing faith in his substantiality, and points out sardonically, in words that might have come from a textbook on mystic discipline: "the belief in God, in all modesty be it said, is sometimes lost following a period of intensified zeal and observance, it appears" (78). As he says wryly, "It is easier to raise a shrine than to bring the deity down to haunt it" (78). Puzzling over whether she has come or not (her name once again becoming Marguerite), he notes he can see no stars. It is truly a dark night; he feels entirely enclosed. "My shadow at evening will not darken the ground" (80), he says, echoing Eliot (*The Waste Land,* l. 29).

A long section follows which might be called variations on the theme of the voices. "They" tell him to be Worm or not to be Worm. "They" fill his mind with thoughts. He is ready to do whatever "they" wish. "They" want to make a man out of dust. Eliot also refers to man as being made of dust (*The Waste Land,* l. 30), but the common source of both allusions is Genesis 2:7: "And the Lord God formed man of the dust of the ground." Again the emphasis is on the analogy between the relationship to his creator (Beckett), and the relationship of man to *the* Creator, emphasized to illuminate not aesthetic problems but metaphysical questions.

The narrator's use of the plural pronoun "they" is deliberately confusing. But that "they" is Beckett is obvious from the comment: "Did they ever get Mahood to speak? It seems to me not. I think Murphy spoke now and then, the others too per-

[19]Although, of course, this vision in turn is probably based on the beatific vision in Ezekiel 1, especially vv. 26–28.

haps, I don't remember, but it was clumsily done, you could see the ventriloquist" (85).

He finally accepts being Worm, and reminds us of "that first disaster, with the appertaining terror and the cerebellum on fire" (87), a reference to his "birth" on the one hand, but on the other to the apparition of the Holy Spirit to the apostles ("And there appeared unto them cloven tongues as of fire, and it sat upon each of them," Acts 2:3).

It took man a long time to adapt to such "excoriation," he declares, to realize life is, in Swift's phrase, "a mere bagatelle" (87). Terrified, he wishes "they" would stop talking (88). Yet he knows very well that "they" is only one voice: "But it's more likely the same foul brute all the time, amusing himself pretending to be a many, varying his register, his tone, his accent and his drivel. Unless it comes natural to him. A bare and rusty hook I might accept" (89). The reference to the hook echoes the previous allusion to God's hooks and plumblines (72). As a concept in the mind of his creator, he is distinctly uncomfortable, and he contemplates sneaking out through the bowels! "They" want him to live, but he knows that life is unpleasant and is reluctant. He begins as an ear, then develops a mouth, and breathes. "They" watch him through a little hole in the wall, and occasionally shine lights upon him (94–95). The voice continues, but he is still convinced it is a single voice. He, that is, Worm, is at the centre and, as Beckett says sardonically, "there is a clue of the highest interest, it matters little to what" (96). It matters more to the reader than to Beckett; as I have said earlier, the centre is associated with God. Worm does not move (98) but "they" want him to move. "They could set a dog on him, perhaps, with instructions to drag him out" (99) echoes Eliot ("Oh keep the Dog far hence, that's friend to man/ Or with his nails he'll dig it up again!" *The Waste Land*, ll. 74–75). The common source is the same Psalm 22 from which comes the reference to being a worm. It is significant that the psalm begins with the words Christ echoed upon the Cross, thus furthering the identification of Christ with all suffering mankind:

> My God, my God, why hast thou forsaken me? why art thou so far from helping me, and from the words of my roaring? O my God, I cry in the daytime, but thou hearest

not; and in the night season, and am not silent. But thou art holy, O thou that inhabitest the praises of Israel. Our fathers trusted in thee: they trusted, and thou didst deliver them. They cried unto thee, and were delivered: they trusted in thee, and were not confounded. *But I am a worm and no man;* a reproach of men, and despised of the people. All they that see me laugh me to scorn: they shoot out the lip, they shake the head, saying, He trusted on the Lord that he would deliver him: let him deliver him, seeing he delighted in him. But thou art he that took me out of the womb: thou didst make me hope when I was upon my mother's breasts. I was cast upon thee from the womb: thou art my God from my mother's belly. Be not far from me; for trouble is near; for there is none to help. Many bulls have compassed me: strong bulls of Bashan have beset me round. They gaped upon me with their mouths, as a ravening and a roaring lion. I am poured out like water, and all my bones are out of joint: my heart is like wax; it is melted in the midst of my bowels. My strength is dried up like a potsherd; and my tongue cleaveth to my jaws; and thou hast brought me into the dust of death. *For dogs have compassed me:* the assembly of the wicked have enclosed me: they pierced my hands and my feet. I may tell all my bones: they look and stare upon me. They part my garments among them, and cast lots upon my vesture. But be not thou far from me, O Lord: O my strength, haste thee to help me. *Deliver my soul from the sword; my darling from the power of the dog.* (Psalm 22:1–20, italics mine)

But no dog would survive, the narrator says; Worm is at the bottom of a pit, and again we have two references to hooks let down (99, 100). The place in which he is is neither hell nor earth. "Perhaps it's the light of paradise, and the solitude, and this voice the voice of the blest interceding. . ." (100). But it is obviously not paradise, and the only "place" left is purgatory. Worm's single eye weeps constantly. The singleness of the eye probably reflects Matthew 6:22: "The light of the body is the eye; if therefore thine eye be single, thy whole body shall be full of light." St. Augustine also refers to the eye of the soul, in the passage on his conversion. As for the constant weeping of the eye, Leclercq points out in *The Love of Learning and the Desire for God* that "the desire for Heaven inspires many texts on tears. The tears of desire, born of the compunction of love, are a gift from Our Lord; they are asked for and their meaning is interpreted . . . these 'tears of charity,' these 'suave tears' " (63). (See also the reference to tears in Elmer O'Brien's *Varieties of Mystic Experience,* 207, in connection with St. Ignatius of Loyola.)

The reason he speaks of his creator as "they" is finally given on page 102: "Worm being in the singular . . . they are in the plural, to avoid confusion." But one realizes "they" is used precisely to confuse the reader. The light, as usual, is grey (103), "but perhaps one day brightness will come, little by little, or rapidly, or in a sudden flood" (104).[20] But at present there is no light and nothing in the greyness, nor does Worm have any notion of time or space. The voices continue, and the narrator continues puzzling over what "they" want. But "they" in their turn, have a master, someone to whom "they" report about what "they" have done with their material (109). When "they" go, the lights will go out and Worm will be in the darkness, but it may not be final. "They" will return and the whole process will start again, including his suffering. A way out would be "to discover, without further assistance from without, the alleviations of flight from self, that's all. . ." (112). But before he can do this, the master summons him through the agent ("they"): "He is there, says the master, somewhere, do as I tell you, bring him before me, he's lacking to my glory" (113). But Worm is incapable of improvement; he cannot say the right words, "the words that will save me, damn me" (114). The messenger goes back and forth to the master, bringing back orders to continue. Sometimes it seems they have "hit the mark"—other times they have to go through it all again, "in other words, or in the same words arranged differently" (116). He desperately wants silence, wants the voice to stop so there will be peace. He says lies have been told to the master, but at this point "they" intervene

---

[20]Cf. Simone Weil, *Waiting for God:* "Even if our efforts of attention seem for years to be producing no results, one day a light . . . will flood the soul" (107–8). See also *Purgatorio* Canto XXIX: "And behold!—/Through all that everlasting forest buried/ An instantaneous flood of radiance."

with some documents, a dossier on a feasible life (125), if only he will agree to accept it and live it. But he refuses, knowing that if he agrees, a long line of descendants will come after him. It would be like the old jingle, the circular one about the dog which is referred to in *Godot*. Nothing, he says, will come of the stories of Worm and Mahood and all the other stories, but if "they" wish, he will shit stories for them, "the daily round and common task" (130), an ironic allusion to Keble's hymn, "New every morning is the love" (No. 260 in the English Hymnal with Tunes, Oxford University Press, 1906), perhaps misremembered by Beckett, for in the original, the words are "the trivial round . . ." The hymn continues: "Room to deny ourselves—a road to bring us daily nearer God." But he has lost the taste for story-telling; he wants only "to wait, without doing anything, its no good doing anything, and without understanding, there's no help in understanding" (131), a perfect description of the mystic passivity. He wants and prefers peace, but "they" prefer a show, a performance.

Since, as we have established, "they" equals Beckett, the creator, and yet the narrator is in some sense also Beckett, what is being described is the conflict between the creative ego and what for lack of a less loaded word we must call the soul. But "there is nothing to be done, nothing special to be done, nothing doable to be done" (137). Yet he cannot attain this serene detachment; he goes on telling stories, suffering, thirsting, cursing.

From here on the monologue becomes desperate in tone, recalling Herbert's line in "The Collar": "But as I raved and grew more fierce and wilde." Paraphrase is extremely difficult, if not impossible, to achieve. The best one can do is to single out various themes and their development, themes which modulate into one another as in music. It must be noted that these variations on given themes are expressed always in a series of paradoxes, so that the effect is of one spinning his wheels to stay in the same place. For example, he says that he is all words and part of all the words and indeed of everything (193), but at the same time he is hard and cold and separate "like a caged beast," a phrase on which many variations are played. We are reminded of Malone's evocation of "the soul in its cage," and of Eliot's phrase in *The Waste Land:* "Each in his prison" (l. 412). Such description of the imprisoned ego or soul is emphatically in the classic Christian tradition. Another long variation is on the theme of seeking (140–142); he seeks yet he does not seek (140) ("Seek and ye shall find," Luke 11:9). Then there is a variation on time (143–144) which "piles up all about you" (144).

On page 145 he notes something has changed. He has for once *not* been talking about Mahood or Worm and regrets the time he has wasted on all the surrogates "till I doubted my own existence," (145) and yet at the same time he wants to lose himself. "Will I never stop wanting a life for myself?" (148). A variation on silence follows (148–154): he may at last be attaining the "true silence . . . the real silence" (149). But he is not, and the usual series of hasty and contradictory statements follow until the theme changes to that of drawing water from one container to fill up another (154–155), which turns into a description of the "place" (157), then into an evocation of morning, which he calls "the dayspring" (repeated twice), and then into a mention of the stable, repeated two or three times. Here we must halt briefly to note that the dayspring is an allusion to Luke 1:76–79 (the entire passage, Luke 1:68–79, is a canticle, the Benedictus, in the *Book of Common Prayer*): "And thou, child, shalt be called the prophet of the Highest, for thou shalt go before the face of the Lord to prepare his ways, to give knowledge of salvation unto his people by the remission of their sins. Through the tender mercy of our God; whereby *the dayspring from on high hath visited us* to give light to them that sit in darkness" (italics mine). In conjunction with the allusion to the dayspring, the word "stable" would seem to be an allusion to the Incarnation, which as we have seen, has been a constant motif in the trilogy, beginning on one of the earliest pages of *Molloy (17)*.

The mention of the Incarnation leads into a passage on the "incarnation" of the narrator: ". . . he seeks me I don't know why, he doesn't come out, he wants me to be he, or another, let us be fair, he wants me to rise up, up into him, or up into another" (163). In other words, this "person" is to be "twice-born." The difficulty is that both he and his creator (Beckett) are ambivalent about his incarnation (164–167), as presumably God the Father was not about that of Christ. Then it is evening, time for a variation on "love" (167), the discarnalized and highly ironic equivalent in *The Unnamable* to the passages dramatizing lust in the other two books.

Back to the silence again and the dark—four pages of it, four pages of ambivalent yearning for silence and peace: ". . . that's not the real silence, it says that's not the real silence, what can be said of the real silence, I don't know. . ." (171). It is a suggestive coincidence that Simone Weil writes about her communion with God while saying the "Our Father": "At times the very first words tear my thoughts from my body and transport it to a place outside space where there is neither perspective nor point of view. At the same time, filling every part of this infinity of infinity, there is a silence, a silence which is not an absence of sound but which is the object of a positive sensation, more positive than that of sound" (72). And again, "To give up our imaginary position as the center, to renounce it, not only intellectually, but in the imaginative part of our soul, that means to awaken to what is real and eternal, to see the true light and hear the true silence" (159).[21]

Can this "real silence" be death, as so many critics suppose? Or the "void, the nothingness" of modern pessimism? I find this impossible to reconcile with the many hints and glancing allusions to a tradition which is far older than any nihilist philosophy, which goes back to Plotinus and the Bible. It is notable, too, that as the intensity of tone increases, the celebrated Beckettian irony fades away. Characteristic of the mystical tradition is the passage about the gleams: ". . . it speaks of tears, then it speaks of gleams, it is truly at a loss, gleams, yes, far, or near, distances, you know, measurements, enough said, gleams, as at dawn, then dying, as at evening, or flaring up, they do that too, blaze up more dazzling than snow, for a second, that's short, then fizzle out. . ." (174). If this is death, then it is death followed by an after-life, which would greatly discomfort the critics who accuse Beckett of nihilism.

Another theme highly characteristic of all mystical religion is

[21]At this point in *Waiting for God*, immediately after talking about the "true light" and "the true silence," Simone Weil uses as an illustration a country road at twilight, and mentions a tree and rustling leaves, a striking analogy between her thought and imagery and that of Beckett in *Waiting for Godot*.

that of the door, as in John 10:9: "I am the door: by me if any man enter in, he shall be saved." Or as in Revelations 3:20: "Behold, I stand at the door and knock: if any man hear my voice, and open the door, I will come unto him, and will sup with him and he with me." The novel ends with a long, extended variation on the theme of the door (174–179), but it ends ambiguously: ". . . if it opens, it will be I, it will be the silence, where I am, I don't know, I'll never know, in the silence you don't know, you must go on, I can't go on, I'll go on" (179).

There is no unitive Vision in the novel. Beckett's narrator achieves Eliot's "unattended Moment, the moment in and out of time," as when Molloy was in the garden at Lousse's, or MacMann has a vision of light on the water, or the narrator of *The Unnamable* sees the gleams. But he does not attain the mystical ecstasy and certainty of Pascal:

> In the year of grace 1654 Monday, 23 November, the day of St. Clement, Pope and Martyr, and others in the Martyrology; the even of St. Chrysogonus, Martyr, and others; from about half past ten in the evening till about half an hour after midnight.
>
> FIRE
>
> God of Abraham, God of Isaac, God of Jacob, not of the philosophers and the learned. Certitude. Joy. Certitude. Emotion. Sight. Joy. Forgetfulness of the world and of all outside of God. The world hath not known Thee, but I have known Thee.
> Joy! joy! joy! Tears of joy.
> My God, wilt Thou leave Me?
> Let me not be separated from Thee for ever.
>
> (The *Pensées*, trans. J. M. Cohen, p. 15)

Nor does he rejoice with St. Augustine:

> And being thence admonished to return to thyself, I entered even into my inward self, Thou being my Guide. . . . I entered and beheld with the eye of my soul above the same eye of my soul, above my mind, the Light Unchange-

able. . . . And thou didst beat back the weakness of my sight, streaming forth Thy beams of light upon me most strongly, and I trembled with love and awe. (Happold, 198)

Yet the last words of *The Unnamable* are, "I'll go on." He will continue to pursue the "real silence."

VI

Nesting in His Branches:
The Quest of Watt

> . . . *it was not an illusion, as long as it lasted . . . that*
> *presence without, that presence within.* . . .
>
> Samuel Beckett

The present study of mysticism in Beckett's work begins with the trilogy of novels because the trilogy first suggested to me the possibility that the mystic quest lay behind the seeming obscurities and peculiarities of Beckett's work. The understanding gained by studying the trilogy in this light enables us now to look backward at *Watt* and *Waiting for Godot* with new eyes and see them as something other than they are popularly supposed to be. In them we see the outlines of stories similar to those in the trilogy, stories of questers who are Christ-figures, mocked and abhorred by many, but still wandering and searching and waiting, in a strangely detached way, for the peace and silence of union with the divine spirit.

Unlike the trilogy, *Watt* was originally written in English, from 1942–44 when Beckett was hiding from the Germans among peasants in the Vaucluse. It is a transitional work in which many of the same ideas and images of the trilogy are expressed, complicated however by the fact that instead of leaving the divine ineffable as he did in *Godot, The Lost Ones, Not I,* and most of the trilogy, Beckett attempted in *Watt* to express it. And, as Arsene says, "any attempt to utter or eff it is doomed to fail" (62). The entire work is based on a typically Beckettian pun—Watt-Knott (what-not in our familiar phrase). So Mr.

Knott accurately embodies the intellectual concepts of God out-
lined by the patristic theologians, but except at rare moments
he comes off as a grotesque, if haunting, figure. Nevertheless,
pace Lawrence Harvey and Martin Esslin, Mr. Knott does stand
for God as "x" stands for apples or nails in an algebra problem.
All the feeling has been left out, as it usually is in algebra
problems. But Knott (Nought) equals the circle of perfection
and infinity which symbolizes God, "Not" is equivalent to the
negative paradoxes by which the mystics express God, "Knot" is
equivalent to Dante's and Eliot's "crowned knot of fire," in
which "the fire and the rose are one."[22] Watt is a Christ figure;
the "what" inherent in the sound of the pun refers to the
incarnation—God—embodied in man. Earlier critics of *Watt*
refused either to recognize Mr. Knott as God or regarded the
portrait as "merely" ironic or at least satiric. But, as usual,
Beckett's irony is far from mere, and it is directed less at the
divine than at man's efforts to conceptualize the divine, which
by definition are self-defeating, as everyone from St. Augustine
to Pascal and beyond has pointed out.

As in *Molloy, Piers the Ploughman,* and *The Divine Comedy, Watt*
begins with the protagonist starting on a journey. Several more
or less realistic persons, to one of whom Watt owes money, are
gathered in a public park discussing Watt. Although this opening chapter is written in the jaunty, jeering style of the earlier
Beckett of *More Pricks* and *Murphy,* these persons describe Watt
in terms which make it clear that he is one of God's blessed
poor and also a figure of Christ. Watt's character is presented
in significantly Biblical terms: "But a milder, more inoffensive
creature does not exist, said Mr. Nixon, He would literally turn
the other cheek, I honestly believe, if he had the energy" (20).
Like Molloy and the other M–questers and like Christ, Watt
has no fixed address ("The Son of Man has nowhere to lay his
head," Matt. 8:20). A Mr. Hackett (representing Beckett himself?) is typically repelled by the open carnality of a couple on
the park bench. After speaking to a policeman about the inde-
cency of this couple, Mr. Hackett is joined by Mr. Nixon and
his wife and they descant severely upon sexuality and procreation, and then give an absurd account of the birth of the

[22]T. S. Eliot, *Four Quartets, Little Gidding,* last two lines.

couple's son. Almost irrelevantly, at the mention of a place called Glencullen, Mr. Hackett says, "It was there I fell off the ladder." It turns out to be a fairly realistic experience; at the age of one he had fallen off the ladder while his mother was out and his father was collecting rock specimens. Yet this casual mention of "falling off the ladder" is a foreshadowing of a more important reference to ladders in Section II of *Watt*.

Then Watt appears, and "Mr. Hackett did not know when he had been more intrigued." He did not know either what it was that so intrigued him. "What is it that so intrigues me, he said, whom even the extraordinary, even the supernatural, intrigues so seldom and so little. Here there is nothing in the least unusual, that I can see, and yet I burn with curiosity, and with wonder" (17). Obviously, there is something striking and significant about Watt. Mr. Nixon reports that Watt is setting off on a journey and points out that when he sees Watt, he thinks of Mr. Hackett, and when he sees Mr. Hackett, he thinks of Watt. Thus Watt, the Christ-figure, is associated with Hackett, who is probably Beckett, just as Molloy, Moran, Malone, and Mahood are all associated with Christ and also with Beckett himself, or at any rate, with the narrator of the stories (see pp. 33, 35, 63, 73 above). The Nixons and Hackett discuss why Watt stopped and got off the train, only to get on it again (it was to pay his debt to Nixon—an action which reminds us of the Biblical injunction: "Therefore, if thou bring thy gift to the altar and there rememberest that thy brother hath ought against thee; Leave there thy gift before the altar and go thy way; first be reconciled to thy brother, and then come and offer thy gift" [Matt. 5:23—24]). Mr. Hackett wants to know more about Watt than Nixon can tell him, but out of his own intuition, Hackett suddenly announces, "He is not a native of the rocks." The phrase is from the eighth eclogue of Virgil, lines 43ff., probably as used by Dr. Johnson in his famous letter to Lord Chesterfield: "The shepherd in Virgil grew at last acquainted with Love, and found him a native of the rocks." Its application to Watt, however, is odd, given that Watt is associated with Christ. Does Mr. Hackett mean that Watt is unloving, or that Mr. Nixon is unloving? Probably the latter. It is interesting that Nixon's wife is called "Tetty," the name of Dr. Johnson's wife, almost as though Beckett wished to be sure we did not miss the reference to Johnson and Virgil. Deirdre Bair quotes Beckett as saying, "They [critics] can put me wherever they want, but it's Johnson, always Johnson, who is with me. And if I follow any tradition it's his" (256).

We leave Mr. and Mrs. Nixon and Hackett, whom we do not see again in *Watt* (although a "Sam" turns up in Section III), and turn to Watt himself, the clown-figure, the holy fool, who is going on a railway journey.

From time immemorial, the journey or pilgrimage has been a metaphor for the human soul's search for the divine ground of being. Far from ceasing when the Industrial Revolution arrived, the metaphor took fresh impetus from railroads, as, for example, Hawthorne's *The Celestial Railroad* attests. Significantly, given the influence of Eliot upon Beckett as accepted, the image of the railway trip as pilgrimage occurs in the *Dry Salvages,* Section III, almost immediately after the lines about "the way up is the way down":

> When the train starts, and the passengers are settled
> To fruit, periodicals and business letters
> (And those who saw them off have left the platform)
> Their faces relax from grief into relief,
> To the sleepy rhythm of a hundred hours.
> Fare forward, travellers! not escaping from the past
> Into different lives, or into any future; . . .

Watt's strange smile is described, a smile that "resembled more a smile than a sneer, for example, or a yawn" (25). It had the effect on the porter, as unearthly innocence usually does, of irritating him and making him hustle Watt. However, Beckett notes that "there were connoisseurs on whom the exceptional quality of Watt was not lost, of *his entry, his fall, his rise,* and subsequent attitudes" (25, italics mine). The curious choice of the italicized words, "entry, fall, rise," seems to suggest either Adam or Christ, or both, and indeed in theology Christ and Adam are often associated or paralleled. Thus it should not surprise anyone who has read this far and who understands Beckett's curious mode of allegory through devious humor that the newstand dealer approaches Watt with a series of "aborted genuflexions" (26)!

Watt sits backward in the train, a position which is probably symbolic of the paradoxically negative approach of the mystics ("In order to arrive at what you are not/You must go through the way in which you are not," *East Coker*, Section III, paraphrasing St. John of the Cross). Watt is watchful; he had once missed the station he is attempting to reach because he was not prepared in time to get off. This line is little frequented—unsurprising in the modern world—but in the railroad car Watt encounters a character called Spiro, the editor of Crux, a popular Catholic monthly. Spiro is a precursor of Moran in Beckett's *Molloy*, with whom he shares a literal, nit-picking approach to religion. Here again, though the satire is in Beckett's earlier smart-young-man vein, some readers and critics have mistaken the object of the satire, which is directed, not against the divine nor against Christ nor even against religion, but against the literal-minded, vulgar reductionism of so many adherents of faith, including, unfortunately, many churchmen as well as lesser folk. Watt, however, hears nothing of Spiro's ridiculous comments; he is listening to other voices:

> . . . singing, crying, stating, murmuring, thing unintelligible in his ear. With these, if he was not familiar, he was not unfamiliar either. So he was not alarmed, unduly. . . . And sometimes Watt understood all, and sometimes he understood much, and sometimes he understood little, and sometimes he understood nothing, as now. (29)

Watt is not crazy, unless all of us are a little crazy, for everyone at one time or another has concentrated on his inward thoughts to the exclusion of outward stimuli. This inward concentration at the expense of "real life" is of course precisely the goal of mystic contemplation, and though it may be confused with schizophrenia, it is not necessarily the same thing (see above, n.3, p. 18).

As they near the station, Spiro sticks his head out of the window and is driven back by "a great rush of air" (30). Here the air, symbolizing the Holy Spirit, repels the literal and self-obsessed Spiro.

Watt sets out from the train, followed by a Lady McCann, whose character is one of the many satiric attacks by Beckett upon the typical hidebound conventional female of a certain age (she reappears as Lady Pedal in *Malone Dies,* for instance). In a reversal of the story of the woman taken in adultery ("let him who is without sin cast the first stone"), she throws a stone at Watt. It bounces off his hat, but Beckett notes that Watt has a wound in his right side—a further identification of Watt with Christ. Watt is accustomed to such attacks, which he receives without resentment, merely staunching the blood, if there is any, with "the little red sudarium" (32) he carries in his pocket. According to the *Shorter Oxford Dictionary,* a sudarium is a handkerchief used to wipe sweat or tears from the face, especially the cloth used by St. Veronica to wipe the face of Christ—still more identification of Watt with Christ. Feeling weak, Watt crouches by the side of the road in the Belacqua posture, "his knees drawn up and his arms on his knees and his head on his arms" (33). Here the identification with Christ ends, for Christ was no Belacqua, and we realize that Watt is only a "little Christ," or Christian. He rests for a time, as Molloy does in the book of that name before entering the town, "listening to the little night-sounds in the hedge behind him. . . "(33). Then he rolls over and lies in the ditch, hearing, like Malone in his solitary room, the sound of a choir. Unlike Malone's choir, which is singing or rather bawling the "Hallelujah Chorus," Watt's choir is singing gibberish, possibly concealed messages from members of the choir to each other. Watt crawls on to Mr. Knott's house and enters, in some confusion, not sure how he got in. He had gone to both doors, front and back, to find them both locked, yet suddenly he is inside the kitchen. This unawareness of how he came into the divine milieu would appear perfectly natural to anyone who has studied the writings of the mystics, for these transactions of the spirit take place suddenly and noiselessly when the persons concerned are least aware.

Suddenly Beckett notes that everything is red—Watt's hair, the kitchen floor, the ashes in the fire which flare up. The only other character in Beckett's oeuvre who has red hair is the woman vanquished in *The Lost Ones,* whom, for reasons which will be explained in the chapter on that work, I take to symbolize the church. Red is commonly associated with the church, because of the scarlet robes of cardinals, and because of the red vestments worn at Pentecost and, in the Anglican church, at

Passiontide. Red is also, of course, the color of blood, fire, and wine, all things of great symbolic significance in the life of the church.

Arsene, the servant Watt is to replace, enters and delivers a long monologue about the time he has spent in service to Mr. Knott. Part of this monologue is nastily jeering in Beckett's early manner, part of it is another attempt to "eff" the ineffable. For example, the following appears to be a description of the mystical state, very similar to passages in *Molloy:*

> . . .the little sounds that demand nothing, ordain nothing, explain nothing, propound nothing, and the short necessary night is soon ended, and the sky blue again over all the secret places where nobody ever comes, the secret places never the same, but always simple and indifferent, always mere places, *sites of a stirring beyond coming and going, or a being so light and free that it is as the being of nothing.* How I feel it all again, after so long, here, and here, and in my hands, and in my eyes, like a face raised, a face offered, all trust and innocence and candour, all the old soil and fear and weakness offered, to be sponged away and forgiven! Haw! Or did I never feel it till now? Now when there is no warrant? Wouldn't surprise me. *All forgiven and healed.* For ever. In a moment. (40, italics mine)

The phrase "all forgiven and healed" is obviously a reference to the redemptive action of the divine grace, as at Holy Communion (though not necessarily at that rite only). Arsene comments that "All the old ways" led to this, "all the old windings, the stairs with never a landing that you screw yourself up" (40). This passage and many others about stairs in *Watt* remind us, not only of the ascending ridges in Dante's *Divine Comedy*, but also of the many similar passages in Eliot, for example in Section III of *Ash Wednesday* ("At the first turning of the second stair/I turned and saw below/The same shape twisted on the banister. . . . At the second turning of the second stair/I left them twisting, turning below . . .").

Arsene remarks that Watt is not quite clear how, "having found the neighborhood, he found the gate, and how having found the gate, he found the door, and how having found the door he passed beyond it" (all Biblical allusions—see Matt.

7:14, John 10:9, Rev. 3:20). Arsene describes the sensations of peace and harmony Watt will feel, "when in a word he will be in his midst at last, after so many tedious years spent clinging to the perimeter"—a reference to the definition of God as a circle whose center is everywhere to which Beckett also alludes in *The Unnamable* (see above, p. 70). In spite of the jeering note in "masturbating his snout" (40) and in "the long joys of being himself, like a basin to a vomit" (41) (what Kenner calls wittily "a juvenescent smartness" in his *Samuel Beckett: A Critical Study*, p. 53), the tone of the whole description of the state of mind awaiting Watt has the lyrical yearning note so often found in the later work, the trilogy, where it is unadulterated by the jokes and satiric phrases. It is significant that the later novels approach the same theme—the pursuit of the divine—with less of this jaunty, almost embarrassed humor, especially in those passages which attempt to "eff" the ineffable.

There will be some labor for Watt in serving Mr. Knott, but he will do it gladly since the work will enable him to "abide as he is, where he is, and that where he is may abide about him, as it is" (41). The use of the biblical word *abide* indicates the hidden context, whether it is John 15 or the familiar words of the hymn (number 363 in the *English Hymnal* of 1906), probably familiar to Beckett from his childhood: "Abide with me; fast falls the eventide;/ The darkness deepens; Lord, with me abide." Watt's regrets will pass "into the celebrated conviction that all is well or at least for the best" (41, cf. Rom. 8:28).

Arsene's description of Watt calmly and gladly peeling the potatoes and emptying the night stool recalls a famous medieval mystic, Brother Laurence, and his *Letters and Conversations on the Practice of the Presence of God,* published in France in 1692: "I turn the cake that is frying in the pan for love of Him . . . It is enough for me to pick up but a straw from the ground for the love of God."

But the sensation of union with the absolute does not last, and Arsene himself went through what he calls "the change." "Something slipped" (42) right in the midst of an extraordinary mood of union with all things: "I felt I had been transported . . . to some quite different yard, and to some quite different season, in an unfamiliar country" (43–44). "But in what did the change consist? What was changed and how? . . .

What was changed was existence off the ladder. Do not come down the ladder, Ifor, I haf taken it away" (44). Much has been made of this statement in a philosophical context and an attempt has been made to align it with the philosophy of Wittgenstein. However, according to John Fletcher, Beckett himself has stated that he has only read Wittgenstein recently (*Samuel Beckett's Art*, p. 136). It is far more likely that the ladders which occur so frequently in Beckett's work begin with Genesis 28:12 (Jacob's ladder), continue with Augustine's "ladder" in Confession XIII (see John Fletcher, *Samuel Beckett's Art*, p. 125), with all the ascents and descents in Dante, including especially the Golden Ladder of the Contemplatives in Paradiso XXI, and have their most recent referent in the ladder of St. John of the Cross made familiar to modern readers by Eliot in the figure of the ten stairs in Section V of *Burnt Norton*.[23]

Arsene points out that even though he lost touch with the divine absolute or, as the mystics would say, entered into a period of aridity, still "it is useless not to seek, not to want" (44). But, in his opinion, "it was not an illusion, as long as it lasted, that presence of what did not exist, that presence within, that presence between" (45), although this statement ends with the customary deflation: "though I'll be buggered if I can understand how it could have been anything else" (45).

From the assertion that the "presence" was not an illusion, Arsene turns away to a passage of jeering farce in the best Beckettian manner, in which he declares the world to be an ordure, an excrement, a turd (46–47). Nevertheless, although the passage appears to be typical twentieth-century nihilism, and the violence of expression is extreme, the pejorative approach to earthly things is well within the classical mystical tradition, from Plato to Swift.

Arsene says that his present feeling is one of sorrow: "This hour is my last on earth in Mr. Knott's premises, where I have spent so many hours, so many happy hours, so many unhappy hours, and—worst of all—so many hours that were neither

[23]Davis Hesla has linked Watt with St. John Climacus' *The Ladder of Divine Ascent*, trans. Lazarus Moore, introd. M. Heppel (New York: Harper and Brothers, n.d.). There may well be a link, but I would rather say that the "ladder" image is common in the Christian mystical tradition.

happy nor unhappy [implication of spiritual apathy, or *akedia*], and that before the cock crows my weary little legs must be carrying me as best they may away" (49). In spite of the reference to the cock, however, Arsene has not denied the validity of his experience. He wishes to be turned into a stone pillar; extraordinarily, critics see this as the typical twentieth-century obsession with emotional numbness, without apparently ever connecting it with Genesis 19, in which Lot was spared destruction on condition that he not look back, but in which his wife, who did look back, was turned into a pillar of salt. Similarly, it is useless and destructive for Arsene to look back to the happy hours he spent in Knott's establishment. The grace has vanished, yet he does look back with longing.

There follows the grotesque tale of Mary, the greedy parlor-maid who eats continuously all day long, a set piece on a par with the sucking-stone routine in *Molloy*. Stripped of the grossly comic description of her eating, Mary appears to be "opposed to conversation" (52), "attached to rest and quiet" (54), and having a "dreamy face," (55), all of which suggests some connection with Mary the sister of Lazarus who did not help Martha with the housework but sat at the feet of Christ, listening to his words (Luke 10: 38–42). Since in so many ways *Molloy* appears to be a recasting of some of the same material, it is interesting that Martha (the name of Mary's sister) turns up in the Moran section of *Molloy*.

Arsene quotes the Anglican hymn "Now the day is over/ Night is drawing nigh" (number 603 in the *English Hymnal* of 1906, written by Sabine Baring-Gould in 1865) (57), and speaks of Watt in Heraclitean terms: "And then another nightfall and another man come and Watt go, Watt who is now come, for the coming is in the shadow of the going and the going is in the shadow of the coming, that is the annoying part about it. And yet there is *one who neither comes nor goes*, I refer I need hardly say to my late employer, but seems to abide in his place, for the time being at any rate, like an oak . . . and we *nest a little while in his branches*. Yet come he did once, otherwise how would he be here, and go sooner or later I suppose he must, though you wouldn't think it to look at him" (57, italics mine).

Knott, incidentally, is attached to a few servants only, all of whom are seedy and shabby. It is frequently pointed out in the

New Testament that the poor are often the truest servants of God, especially cherished by Him; this appears most clearly in the twelve disciples who were seedy and shabby and obviously few in number. Yet "there is something about Mr. Knott that draws towards him" (John 12:32: "and I . . . will draw all men unto me") the seedy and shabby (60–61), in other words, chiefly the poor, oppressed, and outcast, who are "eternally turning about Mr. Knott in tireless love" (62), a phrase which recalls Dante's description of God in Canto XXVIII of the *Paradiso.*

But now Arsene hears "a little wind come and go" (62), just as Molloy does; it is the wind of the divine spirit, and he must leave the house of Mr. Knott. Whether this departure is death or a period of aridity and lapsing from the household of the faith is not clear; however, Arsene feels content that he has said enough "to light that fire in your mind that shall never be snuffed" (62). Just as in *Molloy* and in the Bible, the wind and fire signify theophany, revelation of the divine.

According to Arsene, "Erskine will go by [Watt's] side to be [his] guide," an allusion to the medieval morality play in which Good Deeds offers to go with Everyman on his journey to the grave. The emphasis in *Everyman,* as it also is in so much of Beckett's work, is on death and judgment; the subtitle of the play is "A Treatise how the Hye Fader of Heven sendeth Dethe to Somon every Creature to come and gyve a counte of theyre lyves in this Worlde." Arsene continues, proving the point, ". . . and then for the rest you will travel alone, or with only shades to keep you company" (63). Thus it does appear that leaving Mr. Knott's establishment means death and judgment; we should not be surprised when after leaving Mr. Knott's house in his turn, Watt is discovered in a "mansion" ("In my father's house are many mansions," John 14:2), even though, confounding the literal-minded twentieth-century reader, the "mansion" is rendered suspiciously and jocularly like an institution for the mentally ill. Arsene's final remarks take the form of a "confiteor": "Now for what I have said ill and for what I have said well and for what I have not said, I ask you to forgive me. And for what I have done ill and for what I have done well and for what I have left undone, I ask you also to forgive me. And I ask you to think of me always—bugger these buttons—

with forgiveness, as you desire to be thought of with forgiveness, though personally of course it is all the same to me whether I am thought of with forgiveness or with rancour, or not at all. Goodnight" (63). The remark about "it being all the same to me whether I am thought of with forgiveness or with rancour" is the kind always seized on by Beckett critics as satiric deflation. To be sure, it may, to Beckett's private amusement, appear to be merely deflation, but it also expresses the perfect indifference and calmness with which the contemplative soul faces the changes and chances of this mortal life—an indifference very difficult to achieve in the twentieth century.

Arsene goes, but reappears, somewhat as Christ went but reappeared to his disciples, only Arsene reappears as "two men standing sideways in two kitchen doorways looking at him" (63). Perhaps this double vision is another of Beckett's attempts to mislead his readers by suggesting diplopia as well as resurrection. In any case, more important to Watt and therefore probably to Beckett and to the reader is the dawning of a new day: "first the grey, then the brighter colours one by one, until getting on to nine a.m. all the gold and white and blue would fill the kitchen, all the unsoiled light of the new day, of the new day at last, the day without precedent at last" (64). So much emphasis on the new day should make us suspicious of some underlying meaning. Undoubtedly this "new day", especially associated with the liturgical colors of Easter, gold and white, and the virginal color, blue, has some relationship to the "new man" and the "new life" so often spoken of in the New Testament (2 Cor. 5:17, Eph. 4:24, Rev. 21:5).

Thus, at the end of Section I, we have seen what is essentially the conversion experience. In spite of the jokes and banter and ridicule, the outlines of the story are clear. A gentle diffident soul named Watt, who is also a kind of everyman and a kind of Christ (a "little" Christ, perhaps, as Christians are enjoined to be, or used to be enjoined to be), has undertaken the great quest journey for his soul's health and has come to the establishment of Mr. Knott to enter into his service. That Knott's house is "the household of the faith" goes without saying. Watt listens to the "witness" of another pilgrim servant, Arsene, who tells him that "the presence" is real, even though it may appear to be an illusion, and that we "nest a little while in his branches" (57).

Section II describes Watt's stay in Knott's house and here, under a surface of jeering, even of gross blasphemy, there are cunningly concealed references to the rituals of the church. Like the Albigensians and Cathars, whom he often resembles in his Manichean approach to sexuality and procreation, Beckett conceals one meaning under another. As Beckett says, "even where there was no light for Watt, where there is none for his mouthpiece, there may be light for others" (69). Significantly, in the pages describing Mr. Knott's food (88–96), certain words occur which are basic to any discussion of the Holy Communion: "elements," "fraction," and "red light."

Before discussing these, however, let us consider Watt's first tasks. He is to empty the slops, "not in the way the slops are usually emptied, no, but in the garden" (67), and then all the kinds of flowers on which the slops are dumped are listed in the usual quasi-humorous Beckettian manner. The word "slops" is characteristically misleading to the modern reader, firmly set in his realistic view of Mr. Knott as a "real" person with "real" slops. But there is only one place in the world where slops are ordered to be returned directly and separately to the earth, and that is in the Catholic church (Roman and Anglican) where the water used in the ablutions after Mass is drained away to the earth in a special basin and drain called a "piscina." The piscinae were frequent in England after the thirteenth century, and above them were the ambries, or repositories for the consecrated elements. Watt is instructed that Mr. Knott's slops are not be commingled with anyone else's slops, precisely the reason for the use of piscinae for the rinse water of the holy vessels.

Watt sees little of Mr. Knott, except when he is taking a meal. If we assume, as I do, that Mr. Knott represents God, then the meal at which Watt "sees" Mr. Knott must represent the Holy Communion. Sometimes Watt sees him passing through the dining-room (sanctuary) on his way to and from the garden. These glimpses of Knott may refer to the morning and evening prayer services, or to the side Altar of Repose which represents the Garden of Gethsemane in the Holy Thursday liturgy (see Alan Watts, *Myth and Ritual in Christianity*, p.151). Given Beckett's near-obsession with Good Friday and Holy Week generally, the latter is the more likely explanation. Actually, of course, Watt does not literally see Mr. Knott even in the "dining-room," although he (Watt) is responsible for the dining-room and for preparing Knott's meals.

Few strangers enter Mr. Knott's establishment, and those who do are curious indeed: the gardener, named Mr. Graves (perhaps a grave-digger?), the fishwoman, the postman, and on one important occasion, a father and son named Gall, who come to tune the piano. While all these figures most probably have symbolic or mythic significance which remains impenetrable to me at present, their importance seems to lie in their effect on Watt's mind. The incident of the Galls continued to unfold, in Watt's head, "from beginning to end, over and over again, the complex connexions of its lights and shadows, the passing from silence to sound and from sound to silence, the stillness before the movement and the stillness after, the quickenings and retardings, the approaches and the separations, all the shifting detail of its march and ordinance . . ." (72).

Like all religious mystics still living in the outer world, Watt seeks to penetrate the inner or spiritual meaning of all that he encounters. Previously he had lived at face value (73); now "a thing that was nothing had happened," "with all the clarity and solidity of something" (76). To a mystic the comings and goings of persons are "nothing," but Beckett is careful to indicate that Watt is not insane; he has reported on these incidents to someone, presumably Sam: "For the only way one can speak of nothing is to speak of it as though it were something, just as the only way one can speak of God is to speak of him as though he were a man, which to be sure he was, in a sense, for a time, and as the only way one can speak of man, even our anthropologists have realised that, is to speak of him as though he were a termite" (77). But it was long before Watt learned to accept that a "nothing" had happened; for a very long time he continued to struggle with spiritual or other "meanings" of incidents, instead of merely accepting them with the detachment of the true mystic.

The matter of Mr. Knott's meals lends further support to the notion that we are dealing in *Watt* not with realistic meals, but with a symbolic expression of the Holy Communion: ". . . a single good thing that was neither food, nor drink, nor physic, but quite a new good thing, and of which the tiniest spoonful at once opened the appetite and closed it, excited and stilled the thirst, compromised and stimulated the body's vital functions, and went pleasantly to the head" (87). Watt's job is to prepare the elements of the "single good thing" (the liturgical word "elements" is used on p. 88); in other words he is a priest, or at the very least an acolyte or server at the Mass. The uneaten remains of the meal are given to a neighborhood dog. In the Mass the priest consumes the priest's host first, then the smaller hosts are given to the faithful. Beckett's reason for consigning the fragments of Knott's "meal" to the "dog" appears characteristically ironic and misleading, but probably depends on Christ's statement to the woman at the well: "It is not meet to take the children's bread and to cast it unto the dogs" (Mark 7:27). Jesus is here implying that the children's bread (i.e., the sustaining benefits of the faith) should not be given to those outside the Jewish faith. In Christendom, however, the "children's bread" is given to "the dogs," i.e., to non-Jews and often to persons of little or no faith.

In Mr. Knott's establishment, the presence of a left-over meal (or, if our surmise is correct, consecrated hosts) is indicated by the red light (96), just as it is in the Anglican (High) Church where the reserved sacrament is kept in the ambry, a little cupboard in front of which hangs a red light which is lit only when the ambry contains consecrated elements. Twenty-two pages, more or less humorous, are taken up with Watt's absurd surmises and speculations regarding the fine points of the serving of the meal. Beckett has always satirized theological, or any other, nit-picking (for example, Spiro's speculations regarding the rat which eats the consecrated wafer, or Moran's questions about transubstantiation in *Molloy*). These twenty pages are an example of such satire. Watt's fantastic and bizarre theory leads to an equally bizarre digression on the subject of the Lynch family, supposed supporters of the famished dog. The ten pages devoted to the Lynches portray an absurd family, probably adulterous, plagued by hemophilia and a variety of other ills. With great hesitancy, I offer the speculation that the Lynches symbolically represent the Royal Family, who are the heads of the Church of England and therefore could be said, metaphorically speaking, to support the "famished dog." Be that as it may, the religious vocabulary persists—"grace" on p. 116, "verionica" on p. 117.

The other servant, Erskine, serves Mr. Knott upstairs, a level to which Watt never attains. Erskine often answers a bell in the middle of the night. Curious, Watt eventually penetrates Erskine's room, only to find an extraordinary picture on the wall—the picture of a receding circle containing within it a point (128). Watt wonders: " . . . it was perhaps this, a circle and a centre not its centre in search of a centre and its circle respectively, in boundless space, in endless time, then Watt's eyes filled with tears that he could not stem, and they flowed down his fluted cheeks unchecked, in a steady flow, refreshing him greatly" (129). The picture is an icon representing God, the same image used by St. Augustine (see above, p. 70) and by the medieval mystic Juliana of Norwich (80). But the circle has been breached and is receding, the centre cannot hold, and Watt's eyes fill with tears. In spite of this symbolic evocation of the damage done to the concept of the numinous, "Prolonged and irksome meditations forced Watt to the conclusion that the picture was part and parcel of Mr. Knott's establishment" (130). If further identification of Mr. Knott with God be needed, it is provided on the following page: "as it [Mr. Knott's establishment] was now, so it had been in the beginning, and so it would remain to the end . . ." (131) (see the *Book of Common Prayer*, response to the Gloria Patri: "As it was in the beginning, is now and ever shall be, world without end, Amen").

The basic pattern used by Beckett throughout Watt's stay in Knott's house appears to be a series of comic-bizarre red-herring sequences, each several pages in length, with a religious reference or significance set firmly in the heart of each one. For example, in the midst of a long and frantically mathematical speculation as to the ordering of the servants comes this: " . . . Mr. Knott was harbour, Mr. Knott was haven, calmly entered, freely ridden, gladly left" (135). In the midst of a gross sequence involving Mrs. Gorman the fishwoman (a forerunner of the three old women in the trilogy who mother the protagonists), Watt catches a glimpse of Mr. Knott: " . . . he wished to see Mr. Knott face to face. . . . as Watt's interest in what has been called the spirit of Mr. Knott increased, his interest in what is commonly known as the body diminished. . . . Add to this that the few glimpses caught of Mr. Knott, by Watt, were not clearly caught, but as it were in a glass, not a looking-glass, a plain glass,

an eastern window at morning, a western window at evening"
(146–47; cf. 1 Cor. 13:12).

Just about the time that Watt abandons hope of ever seeing
Mr. Knott face to face, a new servant come to the door, "on a
morning white and soft [when] the earth seemed dressed for
the grave" (148–149). His arrival marks the end of Watt's stay
and when we find Watt again in Section III he is in the "mansion" (John 14:2). As we have already concluded, the transfer
to the mansion represents death and judgment, perhaps even
purgatory. The place is very far from being a hell like Dante's;
it is a garden, or rather a series of gardens, each enclosed by
barbed wire fence and frequented by rats. Watt and Sam, his
friend, only come out and meet "at the call of the kind of
weather we liked, . . . a high wind and bright sun mixed" (153).
As before, the sun and wind are symbols of the divine spirit.
After together mending the bridge over the river and smiling
and giving each other the kiss of peace, Watt and Sam feed the
baby rats to their own fathers and mothers and boast that "on
these occasions . . . we came nearest to God," a statement shocking in itself and even more offensive in a religious parable, if
one is in the habit of thinking of God as benevolent in anthrop-
ormophic terms, God like one of Dickens' rubicund middle-
class philanthropists. But nature *is* red in tooth and claw, and
God not only permits cruelty among animals and men, but
presumably has created its potentiality. Beckett has always
loved to shock, doubtless at first partly for the sheer fun of it,
but also to destroy accepted conventions and stereotypes. The
destruction of the baby rats is a typical example of the Beckettian shock technique. It would be dangerous, however, to regard it as "merely" irony at the expense of God or of our
concept of Him, for any and all concepts of God must eventually come to grips with the facts of necessity, of cause and
effect, of death, early and gratuitous death.

On one occasion Sam sees Watt with bloody face and hands,
bearing an extraordinary "resemblance . . . to the Christ be-
lieved by Bosch, then hanging in Trafalgar Square" (159).
After much effort, Sam is able to draw Watt through a hole in
the fence, and to wipe his face and anoint his face and hands
with ointment, reemphasizing Watt's Christ-like aspect. Then
they walk together "as one man" : "And the sun shone bright

upon us, and the wind blew about us. To be together again, after so long, who love the sunny wind, the windy sun, in the sun, in the wind, that is perhaps something, perhaps something" (163). It is possible that, as in *The Unnamable,* Beckett (Sam) here is analogous to the Creator, and Watt, the child of his brain, to the Son, the wind and sun being evocations of the Holy Spirit.

They are in a little space between the fences, for "we had no common garden any more," a remark I take to be a reference to the post-Reformation fragmentation of the classic Christian tradition. Weird conversations ensue, in which Watt first inverts words in a sentence, then the letters in words, and finally the order of the sentences in a given period. Later he combines all the different inversions. Thus Sam never is sure he has obtained a true and accurate picture of Watt's stay in Mr. Knott's house. The gibberish accounts may parallel the mysteries and discrepancies in the four Gospels, "but in the end I understood," says Sam.

Two digressions follow, one funny one about an aphrodisiac named Bando, the other about Mr. Louit's experience before an Academic Committee. Both of these incidents occurred during Watt's stay at Mr. Knott's house. The Louit-Academic Committee episode is rather tiresome satire and, like Watt, we are glad when Arthur tires of telling his tale. Arthur is tired of the story becaue he wishes "to return, to Mr. Knott's house, to its mysteries, to its fixity. For he had been absent longer from them, than he could bear. . . . For there was no other place, but only there where Mr. Knott was, whose mysteries, whose fixity, whose fixity of mystery, so thrust forth, with such a thrust" (199).

The novel continues with two pages of word-play about Knott's "clothes," which are extremely varied, as one would expect of an anthropomorphic deity. Unexpectedly, the absurd clothing sequence modulates into a description of a spiritual state: " . . . one is in the pit, in the hollow, the longing for longing gone, the horror of horror, and one is in the hollow, at the foot of all the hills at last, the ways down, the ways up, and free, free at last, for an instant free at last, nothing at last" (202), a description of what appears to be a moment of mystic communion.

Knott is again described in the terms of classical theology: "For except, one, not to need, and two, a witness to his not needing, Knott needed nothing, as far as Watt could see" (202). Knott's needing to be witnessed has proved for Hesla and Pilling a stumbling-block to regarding him as an icon of God. However, in the midst of so much religious language as we have in *Watt*, I see no reason not to take the need for witnessing at face value. God, if He exists, will exist forever, but without human witnesses to tell of Him, how will He be known? In that connection, Watt describes his own inadequacy: "But what kind of witness was Watt, weak now of eye, hard of hearing, and with even the more intimate senses greatly below par? A needy witness, an imperfect witness. The better to witness, the worse to witness" (203). The echo of the marriage service, "for better, for worse," is significant, for like all true witnesses, Watt is "married" to Knott.

The next absurd sequence (203–207) is concerned with Knott's movements, ending with Watt's complete assurance that Knott is always with him even when he (Knott) is absent: "But on these occasions Watt, unlike Erskine, did not feel impelled to institute a search, above stairs and below . . . he remained quietly where he was, not wholly asleep, not wholly awake, until Mr. Knott came back" (207). Watt had attained sufficient detachment and confidence that he "suffered neither from the presence of Mr. Knott, nor from his absence. When he was with him, he was content to be with him, and when he was away from him, he was content to be away from him" (207). "So that when the time came for Watt to depart, he walked to the gate with the utmost serenity" (208). However, he does burst into tears in the public road after having left Knott's house.

Before we reach Section IV in which we find Watt on the road, there are two other absurd word-play sequences; these are variations on Knott's voice and speech (208) and on his appearance (209–213). The purgatorial section ends with Watt going backwards through the hole, leaving Sam to follow him with his eyes: "And from the hidden pavilions, his and mine, where by this time dinner was preparing, the issuing smokes by the wind were blown, now far apart, but now together, mingled to vanish."

Section IV of *Watt* picks up where II left off, that is, at Watt's departure from Knott's house, in his strange outfit with which all readers of Beckett are familiar—the baggy pants, the oversize greatcoat, the misfitting boots. Something unearthly in his grotesque and corpse-like appearance appalls a casual onlooker named Micks: "Or was it not perhaps something that was not Watt, nor of Watt, but behind Watt, or beside Watt, or before Watt, or beneath Watt, or above Watt, or about Watt, a shade uncast, a light unshed, or the grey air aswirl with vain entelechies?" (220).

After a walk in the moonlight, Watt arrives at the railway station. He looks back but can no longer see Mr. Knott's house. A word-play sequence introduces another night wanderer, a robed figure (226–227) which reminds us of the robed figure in *Not I*. Wattt cannot tell if the figure is that of a priest or a nun. Eventually the figure fades away and disappears. "Watt seemed to regard, for some obscure reason, this particular hallucination as possessing exceptional interest" (228). He spends the night in the waiting room, amid foul smells and strange apparitions (here perhaps Watt's situation parallels Christ's descent into hell), and in the morning the stationmaster and porter find him there asleep. They douse him with a bucket of water. Lady McCann arrives and they all discuss Watt and his condition. Finally Watt arises and without speaking to the small group gathered around, he asks for a ticket "to the end of the line" (244), which he is given. However, when the train arrives, "it did not take up a single passenger" (245). There is no further reference to Watt in the novel. We may conclude that he has been "translated," or to put it another way, he has "ascended." Mr. Case, Mr. Gorman, and Mr. Nolan look at the East where the sun is rising. A goat appears and walks a way down the road; presumably we may associate this goat with the scapegoat of sacrifice and with Watt (Christ). One of the men "raised high his hands . . ." (245) and the men laugh together at the idea that "they say there is no God" (246). After one last look around for Watt, they contemplate "the hills falling to the plain" (246).

Watt therefore has completed his cycle as a servant of Knott, and in spite of their crude jocularity, the trainmen appear to recognize the numinous quality apparent at his passing.

The fragments appended by Beckett to the novel, where they

are not merely absurd or deliberately misleading, confirm the view of *Watt* as a half-joking but entirely serious parable of the pilgrim life toward God. The last line, "No symbols where none intended" is obviously intended satirically. The whole "novel" is entirely symbolic, with only the faintest approximation of reality at beginning and end. *Watt* is a preview of the spiritual search adumbrated later in the trilogy with less farcicality and less bizarre humor.

The little poem "Watt will not" is an assertion of the validity of the spiritual search:

> Watt will not
> abate one jot
> but of what
>
> of the coming to
> of the being at
> of the going from
> Knott's habitat
>
> of the long way
> of the short stay
> of the going back home
> the way he had come
>
> of the empty heart
> of the empty hands
> of the dim mind wayfaring
> through barren lands
>
> of a flame with dark winds
> hedged about
> going out
> gone out
>
> of the empty heart
> of the empty hands
> of the dark mind stumbling
> through barren lands
>
> that is of what
> Watt will not
> abate one tot

VII

Waiting on God:
The Quest of Vladimir and Estragon

> *I wait for the Lord, my soul doth wait,
> and in His word do I hope.*
>
> Psalm 130

If *Watt, Molloy, Malone Dies,* and *The Unnamable* are parables of
the individual soul's mystic quest, then *Waiting for Godot,* written at about the same general period in Beckett's career, is the
public or cultic equivalent of the same quest. In this play,
instead of the individual and solitary pilgrim, we have four
persons—Vladimir, Estragon, Pozzo, and Lucky—or two, if
each pair is considered to be a pseudocouple. Two people
may not appear to constitute an *ecclesia* or worshipping community, yet we are reminded that when two or three are
gathered under certain conditions, Christ will be among them.
And *Waiting for Godot* is concerned with the fragmentation of
Christendom and with the pathos of those faithful few who
"keep their appointment" in spite of their ignorance and
apathy. Beckett may have enjoyed the critical scurrying to find
a source for Godot in Balzac's M. Godeau, but with our present knowledge of Beckett as an artist who relishes the metaphysical search, it appears that Godot is God. As I have said
above, I assume that the title of the play is an allusion to
Simone Weil's *Waiting for God,* with which Beckett must have
been acquainted at least by reputation. And yet, as will be
seen, the title and the concept could just as easily be derived
from the Bible, especially the Psalms.

However, more important than the identity of Godot is the significance of the tree, which is the only remarkable thing in the stage setting. Those critics who agree that the tree is somehow important to the meaning of the play are loath to equate it with the cross of Christ, still less with divinity or redemption. But, as we have observed, Beckett is virtually obsessed with the cross (see above, p. 35), and with judgment—damnation or salvation. When he sees the cross, he appears always to see also those two other crosses, one on each side of Christ, and the possibilities inherent in each cross.

It is probably unnecessary to explain why the tree in *Waiting for Godot* is no mere natural phenomenon but instead a visual symbol of enormous importance. I have done so in an earlier paper,[24] drawing on many myths—Egyptian, Buddhist, Norse—as recounted in Alan Watt's *Myth and Ritual in Christianity*. Even if we confine ourselves solely to the tree in Christian mythology, there is sufficient evidence to constitute a presumption that Beckett deliberately chose "the" tree to be his setting and symbol. Both the tree of knowledge of good and evil and the tree of life were in the middle of the Garden of Eden, where God used to walk in the cool of the day and where he would rendezvous with Adam and converse with him (Gen. 3:8). In this connection, it is noteworthy that when Pozzo asks Estragon's name, he replies, "Adam" (25). Also Vladimir comments about Godot's visits, "It's always at nightfall" (46).

Tradition has it that Christ's cross was made from wood deriving originally from the tree in the Garden (which one of the two trees is not clear). The mythic-historic legend provided the early church with marvellous correspondences. The tree of knowledge of good and evil or the tree of life—either of which brought death to man—becomes the tree of the Cross which brings eternal life. The words of the prophet use the metaphor of the tree for the coming of Christ:

> There shall come forth a rod out of the stem of Jesse, and a branch shall grow out of his roots; and the Spirit of the Lord shall rest upon him. (Isa. 9: 1–2)

[24]Webner, Helene, "*Waiting for Godot* and the New Theology," *Renascence* XXI (Autumn, 1968), 3–9, 31.

And 1 Peter 2:24 speaks of the cross as tree: "who in his own self bore our sins in his own body on the tree. . . . " In the liturgy, the meaning of the tree reaches a climax in the ceremony of the adoration of the Cross, usually performed on Good Friday, the day Beckett claims as his birthday. One of the oldest hyms in the church, the *Vexilla Regis* of Fortunatus (Hymn 94 in the Anglican Hymnal, 1906) celebrates the cross as tree:

> O tree of beauty, tree most fair,
> Ordained those holy limbs to bear;
> Gone is thy shame, each crimsoned bough
> Proclaims the King of glory now.

Fortunatus' *Pange Lingua* (Hymn 95 in the Anglican Hymnal, 1906) echoes the same thought:

> Faithful cross! above all other,
> One and only noble tree!
> None in foliage, none in blossom,
> None in fruit thy peer may be . . .

Both these hymns were in the 1906 Hymnal in the years when Beckett was growing up. More importantly, both hymns are mentioned admiringly by Stephen Dedalus in Section V of *A Portrait of the Artist as a Young Man* (Viking Critical Edition, 1968, 210). Beckett, who was so close to Joyce and his family, must have been aware of Joyce's fondness for these hymns and of his habit of attending Mass on Holy Thursday and Good Friday, as Stanislaus Joyce recounts in *My Brother's Keeper* (105).

Thus the tree in *Waiting for Godot* can be seen as equivalent to both the Old Testament and the New Testament "trees." Two other references support the significance of the tree as the Cross and as the center of life for the community of the faithful. One is from Revelation: "And the leaves of the tree were for the healing of the nations" (22:2). It would be surprising if Beckett, who appears to know the Bible so well, were not acquainted with this verse. *Purgatorio*, Beckett's favorite book of the *Divine Comedy*, contributes the other reference, from Canto 32, lines 37–60, where the leafless tree bursts into leaf and blossom after the Griffon, symbolizing Christ, ties the chariot (the church), to the trunk of the tree. In *Godot,* of course, the tree only puts forth a few leaves. Still, it is the only live thing in the landscape; the green leaves are the only hope in a desparate quest. Some critics have said that the leaves represent nature's heartless and indifferent persistence in spite of man's tragic existence. Yet no other flowers or shrubs appear, and the countryside is several times referred to as a bog, implying that Beckett wishes to highlight the tree and the tree only.

The "wasteland" atmosphere of the setting of the play also reminds us of T. S. Eliot, whose influence upon Beckett we have taken as a norm throughout this study. It is worth noting here that the tree image is used, along with "waiting on God," in *Murder in the Cathedral:*

> What is the sickly smell, the vapour? the dark green
>   light from the cloud on a withered tree?
>
> (Part I, Chorus)

> Between Christmas and Easter what work shall be done?
> The ploughman shall go out in March and turn
>   the same earth
> He has turned before, the bird shall sing the same song.
> When the leaf is out on the tree. . . .
> . . . .
>   We wait and the time is short
> But waiting is long.
>
> (Part II, Chorus)

Assuming that the tree is deliberately meant as a symbol of the Cross, let us consider how it is used in the text. In Act I, Vladimir and Estragon discuss the situation of the two thieves and the fact that only one Gospel (Luke 23: 39–43) mentions one of the thieves being saved. The theme of the Cross having thus been introduced early in the play, a few moments later Vladimir says that they are to wait "by the tree" (10). The use of the article "the" cannot be an accident, for Beckett made his own translation of the play. This is not just any tree, but "the" tree. They wonder on which day they are to meet Godot, and Vladimir "thinks" it is Saturday. In "Samuel Beckett's Long

Saturday" (included in Nathan Scott's *Man and the Modern Theatre*, 1965), Josephine Jacobsen and William Mueller have made their case for Saturday as the day of "Waiting for Godot," the Saturday on which the shattered and grief-stricken disciples of Jesus scattered in despair, believing their Lord had been destroyed, not knowing what was to come on the morrow. But in the text of the play Estragon replies, "But what Saturday? And is it Saturday? Is it not rather Sunday? [traditionally celebrated as the day of the Resurrection] (Pause.) Or Monday? (Pause.) Or Friday?" At the mention of Friday, traditionally the day of the crucifixion, Vladimir, "looking wildly about him, as though the date was inscribed in the landscape," says, "It's not possible!" Why does he make this strange comment? Because Vladimir, as we shall see later, remembers and understands Christian tradition better than Estragon, although that is not saying very much. Estragon's reply to this is, "Or Thursday?" (11). Thursday traditionally is the day of the institution of the Holy Communion and of the prayer vigil in the Garden of Gethsemane. In the sacrament of Holy Communion Christ is recalled into the midst of the faithful. Thus, if one assumes the day of waiting for Godot is Thursday rather than Saturday, hope is inherent in the anamnesis of Christ in the sacrament. On Thursday also the disciples fell asleep in the garden while their Lord was praying. Likewise, right after this conversation, Estragon falls asleep.

A little later, Vladimir and Estragon contemplate hanging themselves from the tree, but decide to wait and see what Godot says (12a), a clear indication that an ethical norm derived from Godot governs the question of suicide and indeed the conduct of life itself, or they would not be waiting for him (Deut. 30:19: "I have set before you life and death . . . therefore choose life"). The thought of hanging is primarily Estragon's, and it recurs to him again briefly at the end of Act I, but Vladimir, who is the spiritual leader of the pair, ignores him. There are no other references to the tree in Act I.

In Act II, during the night in which the two friends have apparently been parted, the tree has put forth its few leaves. Vladimir is the one who notices the phenomenon: "The tree, look at the tree" (39). They talk about the "dead voices" in stichomythic dialogue about the leaves:

ESTRAGON: All the dead voices.
VLADIMIR: They make a noise like wings.
ESTRAGON: Like leaves.
VLADIMIR: Like sand.
ESTRAGON: Like leaves.
      Silence.
VLADIMIR: They all speak at once.
ESTRAGON: Each one to itself.
      Silence.
VLADIMIR: Rather they whisper.
ESTRAGON: They rustle.
VLADIMIR: They murmur.
ESTRAGON: They rustle.
      Silence.
VLADIMIR: What do they say?
ESTRAGON: They talk about their lives.
VLADIMIR: To have lived is not enough for them.
ESTRAGON: It is not sufficient.
      Silence.
VLADIMIR: They make a noise like feathers.
ESTRAGON: Like leaves.
VLADIMIR: Like ashes.
ESTRAGON: Like leaves.

This poetic dialogue envelops the listeners in a consciousness of the leaves of the tree. The leaves of this tree whisper a message, possibly one which Beckett learned out of fear and pain during the war. Neither living nor dying is enough: There must be something more—a significance beyond mere physical action.

Vladimir and Estragon converse about other things, mainly death (41a) until with a great effort Vladimir recollects himself and returns to the subject of the tree: " . . . let me see . . . ah! The tree!" (42)

ESTRAGON: The tree?
VLADIMIR: Do you not remember?
ESTRAGON: I'm tired.
VLADIMIR: Look at it.
      (They look at the tree.)
ESTRAGON: I see nothing.

VLADIMIR:	But yesterday evening it was all black and bare.
	And now it's covered with leaves.
ESTRAGON:	Leaves?
VLADIMIR:	In a single night.
ESTRAGON:	It must be the Spring.
VLADIMIR:	But in a single night!

Later, they hide behind the tree, which does not suffice to shelter them from the view of Pozzo and Lucky. Still later, they imitate the tree by standing on one leg, more or less unsuccessfully. Those who oppose Christian exegesis of the play declare, as do Jacobsen and Mueller in *The Testament of Samuel Beckett:* "The tree by which Vladimir and Estragon wait will not shelter them, finish them off, or, it seems, be imitated," (64), thus claiming the irrelevance of Christianity in this context. One might guess, however, that Beckett perhaps meant something more subtle—that we cannot hide from the world in Christianity, and that imitating the sacrificial life of Christ is a terribly difficult feat, much harder than mere pious churchiness (i.e., standing on one leg and being a tree). It is probably of some significance here that immediately after Estragon attempts to "do" the tree, staggeringly, he paraphrases the kyrie: "God have pity on me!" (*kyrie eleison:* Lord have mercy upon us).

When Pozzo returns blind and cannot tell where he is, Vladimir refers to the tree (p. 55b):

POZZO:	It isn't by any chance the place known as the Board?
VLADIMIR:	Never heard of it.
POZZO:	What's it like?
VLADIMIR:	(looking around) It's indescribable. It's like nothing.
	There's nothing. There's a tree.
POZZO:	Then it's not the Board.

Pozzo's "Board" has connotations of power, authority, and judgment, and is contrasted with Vldaimir's emphasis on the indescribable place where there is nothing but a tree.

At the end of the play, Vladimir comments, "Everything's dead but the tree." Then Estragon says, looking at the tree,

"What is it?" And Vladimir answers, "It's the tree." The repetition of "the tree" seems purposeful on the part of Beckett.

Considering all these references together, the tree can reasonably be considered the vital element in the play; it is the marker, the sign, the symbol, the meeting-place—"A stage setting for the real action between God and man" (*Interpreter's Dictionary of the Bible*, Vol. 4, p. 697). Or, to quote Rudolf Otto:

> The Cross becomes in an absolute sense the 'mirror of the eternal Father' (*speculum aeterni Patris*); and not of the 'Father' alone—the highest rational interpretation of the holy—but of Holiness as such. For what makes Christ in a special sense the summary and climax of the course of antecedent religious evolution is pre-eminently this—that in His life, suffering, and death is repeated in classic and absolute form that most mystical of all the problems of the Old Covenant, the problem of *the guiltless* suffering of the righteous. . . . The Cross of Christ, that monogram of the eternal mystery, is its completion. Here rational are enfolded with nonrational elements, the revealed commingled with the unrevealed, the most exalted love with the most awe-inspiring 'wrath' of the numen, and therefore, in applying to the Cross of Christ the category 'holy', Christian religious feeling has given birth to a religious intuition profounder and more vital than any to be found in the whole history of religion. (*The Idea of the Holy*, 172–173)

Turning from the subject of the tree to Beckett's pseudocouples, it seems fairly obvious to me that Vladimir and Estragon represent soul and body, however unfashionable that word 'soul' may be. The symbolism of their names—Vladimir, the eleventh-century czar who was converted to Christianity and who is also called Saint Vladimir, and Estragon, the French for the herb tarragon—is an indication that Vladimir is the leader, the consciously reflective one of the two. All through the play it is he, not Estragon, who insists that they are waiting for Godot, and it is he who comments on their situation in spiritual or metaphysical terms. He instantly recognizes that Pozzo is not Godot (15b and 16a), even though he acknowledges that he and Estragon "don't know him [Godot] very well . . . " (16a). Estragon, on the other hand, speaks, thinks, and feels in sensual terms: he is concerned with food, with sleep, with his pain-ful feet. Together they can be seen as one man, the basic Adam of us all, waiting to meet Godot at twilight, just as in the good old days in the Garden of Eden. They are a bit unsure of the place and time—a metaphor for the fact that the divine is "out-side of" space and time. Human measurements are irrelevant to the experience of the divine. Godot communicates with the pair, in a vague and confused way, through the shepherd lad or lads, who have obvious connotations of both the Old and New Testaments (David and Jesus). But Godot does not come to keep his appointment for the evening promenade, at least not during the duration of the play.

The fact that Godot does not come has been seized upon by many critics as grounds for assertion that Godot does not exist and certainly that in Beckett's mind God does not exist. How-ever, as was discussed earlier, God's hiddenness or seeming absence does not necessarily mean his nonexistence and did not mean so in the Bible. Many scriptural texts, particularly in the Psalms, give evidence of the "waiting on God" which is so much a part of religious experience (see Psalms 25, 27, 33, 37, 39, 49, 62, 69, 130). Young's *Analytic Concordance to the Bible* gives one column and a half to references to waiting on or for God, including many other books of the Bible besides the book of Psalms. Since I have had occasion to refer to Herbert earlier as a kind of normative Christian gloss on Beckett, it is worth not-ing that many of Herbert's poems express the anguished long-ing for God to "come," as in these lines from "Deniall":

> As good go any where, they say,
>   As to benumme
> Both knees and heart, in crying night and day,
>   *Come, come, my God, O come,*
>   But no hearing.

Rudolph Otto offers further corroboration of the fact that God's "absence" does not mean his nonexistence:

> We say, then, that this doctrine of the omnipresence of God—as though by a necessity of His being He must be bound to every time and to every place, like a natural force pervading space—is a frigid invention of metaphysical

speculation, entirely without religious import. Scripture knows nothing of it. Scripture knows no 'Omnipresence', neither the expression nor the meaning it expresses; it knows only the God who is where He wills to be, and is not where He wills not to be, the *deus mobilis*, who is no mere universally extended being, but an august mystery that comes and goes, approaches and withdraws, has its time and hour, and may be far or near in infinite degrees, 'closer than breathing' to us or miles remote from us. The hours of His 'visitation' and His 'return' are rare and solemn occasions, different essentially not only from the 'profane' life of every day, but also from the calm, confiding mood of the believer, whose trust is to live ever before the face of God. (*The Idea of the Holy*, 214)

Similarly, Simone Weil's *Waiting for God*, asserts God's initiative: "We are incapable of progressing vertically. We cannot take a step toward the heavens. God crosses the universe and comes to us" (133). The play itself confirms this view, for Vladimir and Estragon have at some previous time communicated directly with Godot (13):

> ESTRAGON: What exactly did we ask him for?
> VLADIMIR: Were you not there?
> ESTRAGON: I can't have been listening.
> VLADIMIR: Oh . . . Nothing very definite.
> ESTRAGON: A kind of prayer.
> VLADIMIR: Precisely.

Note here once again that it is Vladimir (the soul) who received the message; Estragon (the body) wasn't listening. True, the message they received was equivocal and baffling, and Beckett jokes about it through their comments. Nevertheless, Vladimir calmly insists that "we come in . . . on our hands and knees" (13a). In other words, there is no option but to submit to the divine prerogative. In Beckett's typically misleading manner, the phrase "We lost our rights" may be taken to refer to their relationship with Godot, i.e., implying that Godot is a tyrant. However, on the next page, Vladimir asserts that they are *not* tied to Godot, thus establishing the free will basic to Judeo-Christianity. The rights which they have surrendered are probably civil and moral ones, and their loss of these rights is consequent on the Fall and on the resulting secularization of the world.

In comparison with the trilogy, the most interesting aspects of *Waiting for Godot* are twofold: the contrast between the secular world (Pozzo and Lucky) and the faithful (Vladimir and Estragon), and the fragmentation and impoverishment of Christian culture among the "faithful." Pozzo represents the Prince of this world, of whom Christ speaks (John 12:31, 14:30, 16:11). His every action demonstrates his brutal egotism—his Henry-the-Eighth manner of eating, his callousness toward Lucky, his hypochondria, his sentimental, pseudolyrical, patronizing cant (20,22, 25), his insistence that everyone look at him, listen to him, and admire him (20a, 25a). Pozzo offers fatalistic determinism as a rationalization of why he is the master and Lucky the slave: "Remark that I might just as well have been in his shoes and he in mine. If chance had not willed otherwise. To each one his due" (21a). It is noteworthy that Pozzo's allusions are all to pagan antiquity—Atlas and Jupiter (21), Pan (24), the Net (which could be Vulcan's net for Venus and Mars, 27). Such allusions are in contrast to those of Vladimir, which are nearly all Christian allusions to the Bible or the Anglican hymnal. Even Lucky's monologue, grotesque and confused though it is, is concerned with theology and ends with an obsessive incantative repetition of words "the skull, the skull, the skull." The word, "Golgotha," which is the Hebrew name of the place where Christ was crucified, means a skull. Demented though he is, Lucky, like his creator, is obsessed with the crucifixion. Pozzo's reaction to Lucky's declamation is an explosion of rage; he literally cannot bear to be reminded of the event which took place on Golgotha, nor can he bear that the attention of Vladimir and Estragon is given to his slave instead of to himself.

Later in the play, Pozzo becomes blind. Since he can see nothing but himself, it is symbolically accurate that he should become blind. The words of theologian Ladislas Boros in *Hidden God* (Seabury Press, 1973) are singularly appropriate here:

'He who loves his brother abides in the light' (1 John 2:10). Only love opens our eyes and enables us to understand the meaning of life. Thus blindness quite simply means the inability to love. . . . Blindness is the attitude of groping towards, of taking possession of. It does not let the other appear, and refuses him the opportunity to expand. In its desire to be solely in charge, it uncreates creation, and darkens life in the world. Thus it no longer has anything in which it can lose itself and once more find itself. Its own countenance gradually begins to darken, as it turns towards darkness. (29–30)

The second interesting aspect of *Waiting for Godot* is the attention given to the impoverishment of Christian culture. The fact that our popular culture is post-Christian is very evident in the play. Molloy, Malone, and the narrator of *The Unnamable* may speak cryptically and in cypher, so to speak, but they are enormously erudite and fully acquainted with classic Christian tradition, which surfaces frequently in their stories in the form of biblical and other religious allusions. Vladimir and Estragon, however, are ignorant of their roots and have only a very imperfect grasp of their "religion." They are the typical theological illiterates of today, dimly aware that there is more to religion than just keeping an appointment, but not quite sure what "more" should consist of. For example, Vladimir says, "Hope deferred maketh the something sick, who said that" (8). Molloy would have quoted the lines correctly and sardonically referred us to Proverbs 13. When Vladimir suggests they repent, Estragon asks, "Repented what?" (8a), reflecting the confusion which today surrounds the whole notion of sin. Estragon also has only a very hazy and primitive notion of the Bible. In discussing the two thieves, Vladimir has to search for the word "damned," a word not much in use any more. In addition, the bizarre confusion in Lucky's great speech indicates a breakdown or collapse of Western Christian tradition. Decoded, it tells us one thing, that in spite of God, man dies. Vladimir knows very well that man dies, but unlike Lucky, he is aware of another context, represented by the two thieves, in which how one lives is of supreme importance. In his longest speech in the play, Vladimir cries:

Let us do something, while we have the chance! It is not every day that we are needed. Not indeed that we personally are needed. Others would meet the case equally well, if not better. To all mankind they were addressed, those cries for help still ringing in our ears! But at this place, at this moment of time, all mankind is us, whether we like it or not. Let us make the most of it, before it is too late! Let us represent worthily for once the foul brood to which a cruel fate consigned us! What do you say? (Estragon says nothing.) It is true that when with folded arms we weigh the pros and cons we are no less a credit to our species. The tiger bounds to the help of his congeners without the least reflexion, or else he slinks away into the depths of the thickets. But that is not the question. What are we doing here, *that* is the question. And we are blessed by this, that we happen to know the answer. Yes, in this immense confusion one thing alone is clear. We are waiting for Godot to come— (51a & b)

Because Vladimir and Estragon do nothing dramatic, save no lives, perform no miracles of helping and healing, it is tempting to regard the above speech as wholly ironic. But they *do* help each other, and help Lucky and Pozzo, in their modest way. Beckett's use of the Hamlet phrase, "that is the question," may be intended to direct us to life rather than death. In spite of hints to the contrary, "to be or not to be" is *not* the question in *Waiting for Godot*. According to Vladimir, the authoritative voice in the play, "What are we doing here, *that* is the question" (51a). He summarizes what they are doing as "waiting for Godot," but if Godot is God, waiting for Him has enormous consequences in the way one lives.

Why are they waiting for Godot, imperfect and anthropomorphic as their concept of him is? To answer this question, let us review every mention of their reasons for waiting. The first explanation for any reason or motive for waiting is on page 12a. Vladimir says, "I'm curious to hear what he has to offer. Then we'll take it or leave it." According to the Bible, what God has to offer is the Covenant, Old or New. In the Old Covenant the exchange between God and man is a quid pro quo—God's choice of the Jews to be a great people in return for their obedience to the Law (Deut. 4, Exod. 19:4–6). In the New Testament, the grace of God and forgiveness of sins are free gifts to all men because of the sacrificial death of Christ (Rom.

119

5, especially verse 15). Thus what God offers in both cases is his love, mercy, and forgiveness to those who recognize his awe-ful power and majesty. But the conversation between Vladimir and Estragon on page 13 indicates that Vladimir prayed for something—we don't know what—and that God's answer was a temporizing and equivocal one. Nevertheless Vladimir flatly asserts that we come in "on our hands and knees."

When the messenger from Godot comes at the end of Act I and asks what message he should carry back to Godot from them, Vladimir's only answer to "Tell him that you saw us." In other words, they are, as Vladimir says later in the play, keeping their appointment. The latter is the absolute minimum of response to God, but actually Vladimir and Estragon are doing more than the minimum. Vladimir cares for Estragon tenderly, and they both express concern about Pozzo's cruel treatment of Lucky (18–18a, 22a). Even though Lucky viciously kicks Estragon when the latter tries to wipe away his tears—an allusion, incidentally, to the story of Saint Veronica's veil often referred to by Beckett (for example, see above, p. 91)—in spite of this hostile reaction, Vladimir comforts Estragon yet does not repudiate Lucky. After the kicking incident, he defends Lucky to Pozzo once again: "And now you turn him away? Such an old and faithful servant! . . . After having sucked all the good out of him you chuck him away like . . . like a banana skin. Really . . ." (22a). On page 30, Vladimir and Estragon are still concerned about Lucky. Vladimir warns Pozzo, "You'll kill him" and they try to help Lucky to his feet.

In the second act, Vladimir sings a lullaby to Estragon and covers him gently with his own coat, meanwhile walking up and down "swinging his arms to keep himself warm." He reassures Estragon when the latter has a nightmare. When the blind Pozzo falls, Vladimir suggests helping him and makes his big speech, "Let us do something while we have the chance!" Vladimir actually does try to lift the fallen humanity of Pozzo and Lucky. When they finally do raise Pozzo, Estragon says (54a), "He wants to know if we are friends."

Vladimir:	No, he means friends of his.
Estragon:	Well?
Vladimir:	We've proved we are, by helping him.

This exchange appears to parallel the story of the Good Samaritan, in which Christ asked, "Which now of these three, thinkest thou, was neighbour unto him that fell among thieves? And he said, He that shewed mercy on him" (Luke 10:36–37). The fact that immediately after being lifted Pozzo asks if they are highwaymen may be a hint to recall to the reader the story of the Good Samaritan. According to Hesla, the whole of the play leads up to this image, of Pozzo hanging on the necks of Vladimir and Estragon, a moment "which, in its simplicity and purity, stands in judgement on the meaningless waiting, the tyrannical abuse of one's fellowman, and the ravings of a maddened intellect which in the play pass for 'entertainment' " (144).

These caring actions and thoughts on the part of Vladimir and Estragon are causally linked with the flowering of the tree and the other signs of the Presence (the messengers, the sudden appearance of the well-fitting shoes). When the boy comes again and Vladimir ascertains that Mr. Godot has a white beard—a hint therefore that he is indeed the anthropomorphic God of Michelangelo and Blake, of Western tradition—the kyrie is paraphrased for the second time in the play. "Christ have mercy upon us!" says Vladimir. The kyrie is a cry of greeting, of affirmation, and Beckett may have thought that through his use of it in the play he was making his hints of divinity crystal clear.

At the very end of the play, after the boy has come and gone again in the usual enigmatic way, Estragon, who has been sleeping, wakes up and once again suggests they go away. Vladimir reminds Estragon that they must return to the tree because they are waiting for Godot. Estragon asks what would happen if they "dropped him." Vladimir replies succinctly, "He'd punish us" (59a). A few speeches farther on, Vladimir states that if Godot comes, "We'll be saved" (60a).

Thus it seems that they are in contact with Godot, even though during the time frame of the play they have not experienced his Presence in its immediacy; that Godot represents both an ultimate power and an ethical norm; and that in their ignorant, groping way, they are faithful to the little they know or understand of what God means and what He requires of them. This appears to be an accurate picture of the average man-in-the-street's relationship to God in his church. In Beckett's characteristic manner the serious references are embedded in jokes and comic routines, scatological and otherwise. Thus some critics conclude that Beckett is only satirizing religion. Yet a careful reading of *Waiting for Godot* will show, I believe, that the object of satire is not the waiting and longing for Godot. The objects of satire are exactly what they were in *Watt* and in the trilogy: first, sexual desire and its apparatus (through Vladimir and Estragon), then power and brutality (through Pozzo and Lucky), and finally academic pedantry (through Lucky's speech).

When asked what he meant by *Waiting for Godot*, Beckett has given the evasive replies so often offered by serious artists when asked to explain their work. He has said, "If I knew I would have said so in the play," which can be turned around to indicate, "My play says what I know." He has also said, "There is a wonderful sentence in St. Augustine . . . Do not despair, one of the thieves was saved. Do not presume, one of the thieves was damned." This statement explicitly refers to the possibility of damnation or salvation. But in *Waiting for Godot*, damnation or salvation for whom? Most readers would probably agree that Pozzo and Lucky are already "damned," in that their lives are a sadomasochistic hell. The fate of Vladimir and Estragon, however, is by no means so clear. Yet if we turn to the one Gospel which indicates that one of the two thieves was saved, we find that the thief who was saved took the initiative. He rebuked his fellow malefactor who railed at Christ, and he implicitly confessed his sin, saying, "Dost thou not fear God, seeing thou art in the same condemnation? And we indeed justly, for *we receive the due reward of our deeds* . . . (italics mine). And he said unto Jesus, Lord remember me when thou comest into thy kingdom." (Luke 23: 40–42). Thus, although the mystery remains why God's grace fell on this thief and not on that one, the answer for the play is sufficient: Vladimir and Estragon represent the "good" thief and are "saved," for they are waiting for Godot, they acknowledge his ethical claim and admit his power to punish or to save. Vladimir-Estragon are no more morally pure or ethically perfect than the thief; they are common, ordinary men, *l'homme moyen sensuel*, full of faults and vanities. But they have that "one thing needful" (Luke 10:42); they are attentive to the Lord, they are waiting on God by the foot of the Tree of the Cross.

The words of Paul Tillich in *The Shaking of the Foundations* are strikingly parallel to, almost a gloss on, the content of the play:

> The state of our whole life is estrangement from others and ourselves, because we are estranged from the Ground of our being, because we are estranged from the origin and aim of our life. And we do not know where we have come from, or where we are going. We are separated from the mystery, the depth, and the greatness of our existence. We hear the voice of that depth, but our ears are closed. We feel that something radical, total, and unconditioned is demanded of us, but we rebel against it, try to escape its urgency, and will not accept its promise. We cannot escape, however. If that something is the Ground of our being, we are bound to it for all eternity, just as we are bound to ourselves and to all other life. We always remain in the power of that from which we are estranged. That fact brings us to the ultimate depth of sin; separated and yet bound, estranged and yet belonging, destroyed and yet preserved, the state which is called Despair. Despair means that there is no escape. Despair is 'the sickness unto death.' But the terrible thing about the sickness of despair is that we cannot be released, not even through open or hidden suicide. For we all know that we are bound eternally and inescapably to the Ground of our being. The abyss of separation is not always visible. But it has become more visible to our generation than to the preceding generation, because of our feeling of meaninglessness, emptiness, doubt, and cynicism—all expressions of despair, or our separation from the roots and meaning of our life. Sin in its most profound sense, sin as despair, abounds amongst us. (159–166)

But there is a way out of despair for Vladimir and Estragon, at the foot of that tree which recalls God in the form of the suffering servant, the "man for others," as Bonhoeffer described Jesus. Other words of Bonhoeffer suggest strongly the concept of God in *Waiting for Godot:*

> Our relation to God is not a religious relationship to a supreme Being, absolute in power and goodness, which is a spurious concept of transcendence, but a new life for

others, through participation in the Being of God. The transcendance consists not in tasks beyond our scope and power, but in the nearest Thou at hand. [*Vide* Vladimir-Estragon's concern for Lucky]. God in human form, not, as in other religions, in animal form—the monstrous, chaotic, remote and terrifying—nor yet in abstract form—the absolute, metaphysical, infinite, etc.—nor yet in the Greek divine-human of autonomous man, but man existing for others, and hence the Crucified. A life based on the transcendant. (219–220)   237-238

Paul Tillich, in the chapter "Waiting" in the same book quoted above, strikingly expresses the paradox of the mystic's waiting for God (149–150); the book also contains an extraordinary chapter titled "Born in the Grave," a phrase reminiscent of Beckett's "They give birth astride of a grave." Tillich says:

> Waiting is not despair. It is the acceptance of our not having, in the power of that which we already have.
>   Our time is a time of waiting; waiting is its special destiny. And every time is a time of waiting, waiting for the breaking in of eternity. . . . Time itself is waiting, waiting not for another time, but for that which is eternal.

This, I believe, is the meaning of the play.

VIII

The Way Out of the Cylinder:
The Quest for the Lost Ones

*For the passion to search is such that
no place may be left unsearched.*

Samuel Beckett

Like *Watt, The Lost Ones* appears to be an ideogram or literary
diagram of man's epistemological position in the twentieth century—a position rendered by Beckett as despairing, exhausted,
yet curiously persistent toward metaphysical ends. When the
little book first appeared, it was treated with gingerly reverence, no critic wishing to assert meaning a later generation of
graduate students would prove to be "wrong." The title of Paul
West's witty review in the Washington Post of December 24,
1972, is typical: "Hell or Heaven? Hell and Heaven?" Yet Mr.
West does not commit himself one way or another, not in this
review at least, beyond saying that in *The Lost Ones*, Beckett has
scrunched "much of Dante into Plato's cave."

There is an indefinable Platonic resonance to *The Lost Ones*,
given the ladders which are so prominent in this strange enclosed world and the opening phrase, "lost bodies each searching for its lost one," both of which seem to direct the reader to
the *Symposium*. However, both the ladders and the lost ones are
ambiguous herrings characteristically drawn by Beckett across
the trail. The Dante resonance in *The Lost Ones* is far greater
than that of Plato, as one would expect. The *Inferno* and the
Purgatorio are conceived as a series of ascents, and Dante looks
upwards from both to catch a glimpse of the stars. Similarly, in

The Lost Ones, the little inhabitants of the cylinder try to ascend by means of ladders to certain "alcoves." The search for the ladders and the attempt to climb them are all-important.

Leaving aside for the moment "each searching for its lost one," the first allusion we run across on the very first page of *The Lost Ones* is: "Inside a flattened cylinder fifty metres round and eighteen feet high *for the sake of harmony . . .*" (italics mine). This seemingly meaningless phrase is repeated at intervals throughout the first part of the fable:

> They [the ladders] are propped against the wall without regard to harmony. (9)

> For half the rungs are missing and this without regard to harmony. (10)

> They [the alcoves] are disposed in irregular quincunxes roughly ten metres in diameter and cunningly out of line. Such harmony only he can relish. . . . (11)

Other allusions to harmony appear on pages 16 and 17. So many repetitions in the work of so careful a craftsman argue some significance. It is true that Plato speaks much of harmony in the *Symposium* and in the *Republic.* These references, how-ever, are to the specific role of harmony in love or in educa-tion, rather than to its ontological role in philosophy generally. John Fletcher in *Samuel Beckett's Art* (136) has pointed out allu-sions in *Murphy, How It is,* and *Molloy* to Leibnitz's "pre-established harmony," and the references in *The Lost Ones* may be satiric comments on Leibnitz's philosophy. Or they may be to Heraclitus, with whom we know Beckett to be familiar. He alludes to Heraclitus in *Murphy, More Pricks than Kicks,* and in *Waiting for Godot.* The most famous single line of Heraclitus— "the road up and the road down are one and the same"—was made famous by T. S. Eliot in his *Four Quartets* and is alluded to by Beckett in *Watt* (202). Harmony in Heraclitus is the unity resulting from the conflict of opposites. Finally, the allusions to harmony may be straightforward allusions to the heavenly har-mony of all the arrangements in Dante's cosmos.

The next few lines of *The Lost Ones* (7) describe the light, which is "omnipresent." The use of this word, so often applied to God in traditional theology, is significant. "Light" as commonly used by all mystics, including Dante, and by T. S. Eliot and Beckett himself, certainly refers to the divine. Dante repeatedly stresses that he and Virgil travel toward the sun and the other stars, which symbolize God. When the restless light inside Beckett's cylinder is stilled, "all go dead still" (7) for a few seconds, then all begins again as the light begins once again to oscillate with a regular beat. Thus the life of the universe of the cylinder is sustained by the stroke of light as God sustains the world in classical Christian theology. In a similar manner, the temperature of the cylinder also fluctuates. The description of the light, the pulse of temperature, and the momentary stoppage of both recalls the descriptions of time and eternity in both Boethius' *Consolation of Philosophy* and Plato's *Timaeus*. The light, of course, is dim, as the divine light would be dimly apprehended by mortals, and eventually the vision of all deteriorates because of the murky gloom. Beckett notes that one might assume, incorrectly, that the vanquished are blind, but they are not. In the cylinder there is also a simple sound "as of insects" (38) emitted by "the light itself and the one invariable." The light has no apparent source; it permeates the entire space. The ladders themselves seem to emit light. The inequity between the oscillations of light and temperature is explained as being necessary for the needs of the cylinder, "so all is for the best," probably a satiric reference to Voltaire's Dr. Pangloss.

When the oscillation is cut off, so is the temperature, "as though the two were connected somewhere to a single commutator" (42). The choice of this word is typically Beckettian in its ambiguity, and may throw the reader off the scent, unless he checks its meaning in the Shorter Oxford Dictionary. Here we find that a commutator is "a contrivance for altering the course of an electric current." So far, so good, or at least so realistic. But the secondary meaning of "commutator" is "he who or that which commutes," which verb can be related to punishment and thereby conceivably indicates a divine presence or judge. But what, where, or who the "commutator" is must remain a mystery: "For in the cylinder alone are certitudes to be found and without nothing but mystery"(42). (See 1 Cor. 15:51: "Behold I show you a mystery.") And on a later page, "All has not been told and never shall be" (51).

The account of the physical properties of the cylinder is written with the usual Beckettian attention to mathematical precision and detail, like the sucking-stone routine in *Molloy* and many other similar passages in Beckett's work. We must remember, however, that the *Divine Comedy* is also worked out with extreme precision and attention to mathematical detail.

The ladders are not arranged in harmony, and half of their rungs are missing, again disharmoniously. Perhaps this disharmony indicates that the ladders are the works of the creatures in the cylinder, as opposed to the harmonious work of the "commutator." Much has been made of ladders in Beckett's fiction, and various philosophic interpretations have been given of his use of ladders.[25] However, as has been pointed out, if Dante is the presiding inspiration of *The Lost Ones*, as he is of Beckett's work generally, we do not need to look any further for an explanation of the ladders which provide for ascent in Beckett's cosmos as the stairs and ridges do in Dante's world.

"The need to climb is . . . widespread. . . . To feel it no longer is a rare deliverance," the author comments wryly (10). A "happy few" (alluding to Shakespeare's golden-boy militarists in *Henry V*) use the missing rungs to "brain themselves," but at best these efforts produce only brief respites from the search. The ones who try to brain themselves remind us of a long succession of Beckettian protagonists who attempt to still the restlessness of the metaphysical quest in some drastic way, by rocking (*Murphy*), hanging (*Waiting for Godot*), and other such devices. If the ladders represent the metaphysical quest, as I believe they do ("it was the custom not to climb two or more at a time," as one does not attempt to follow two or more philosophies or religions at a time), then the niches or alcoves probably represent the havens of various religions, philosophies, or other value-systems explaining the meaning of life. We remember that in *Molloy*, after leaving the house of Sophia (Wisdom), the quester is tempted to remain in a littered blind alley, also called an alcove.

The niches are disposed in irregular quincunxes, which are "cunningly out of line" (11), but apparently *in* harmony. Beck

[25]See Ruby Cohn, "Philosophical Fragments in the Works of Samuel Beckett," in *Samuel Beckett: A Collection of Critical Essays,* ed. Martin Esslin (Englewood Cliffs, N. J.: Prentice Hall, Inc., 1965), p. 174.

ett points out that anyone who could have a total overview of all the niches (i.e., of all metaphysical systems and beliefs), would see that they are in harmony, but that "each climber has a fondness for certain niches and refrains as far as possible from the others" (12). These quincunxes are possibly an allusion to Sir Thomas Browne, yet another of the men of science who, like Descartes and Pascal so dear to Beckett, affirm the mystical side of Christianity in spite of their scientific bias and training. In *The Garden of Cyprus,* Browne describes the quincunx—a way of planting four trees in a circle with one in the center. If a line be drawn bisecting the circle of trees, through the central tree .and again at right angles, as described by Browne (Everyman edition, 194), we have the cross, whether the cross of Christ or that of St. Andrew. The cross being virtually an obsession with Beckett, understandable in one who claims to be born on Good Friday, one feels the connection with Sir Thomas Browne (and therefore with Christianity) to be more than tenuous.

It is not clear whether the world of the cylinder symbolizes individual death or the end of the world. It is a "last state," however, when "light and climate will be changed in a way impossible to foretell" (15), a seeming allusion to St. Paul: " . . . we shall not all sleep, but we shall all be changed" (1 Cor. 15:51). It is to be noted that the way into and the way out of the niches are one and the same (12), as in the writings of Heraclitus, St. John of the Cross, and T. S. Eliot, and some are connected by tunnels (perhaps symbolizing historical connections between various metaphysical or religious systems?).

Inhabiting this world of ladders and niches are several kinds of searchers: the active searchers, the searcher-watchers, the sedentary, and the vanquished. The sedentary sit in "the attitude which wrung from Dante one of his rare wan smiles" (14). This attitude, of course, is the Belacqua posture of cynical despair and indolence (*Purgatorio,* Canto IV, 11. 103–135), which so preoccupies Beckett and which appears in one form or another in almost every one of his works. Beckett points out, however, that the sedentary searchers can still occasionally flash into a moment of passionate concern before subsiding into their typical indolence. Most of the searchers are indifferent to fraternity, not helping each other and occasionally exploding into violence against each other. Conventions govern the use of the ladders—presumably these conventions symbolize either academic conventions or those of sects and denominations or both. The ladders (systems) must be at the free disposal of all, and Beckett outlines an elaborate "climbers' code" (27). Along the wall is a belt one meter wide reserved for the carriers of ladders, and one cannot help but see this belt and its occupants as a satire of metaphysicians and theologians in the finest Swiftian manner. In this belt are a number of "semi-sages," or "sedentary searchers" who are proud and quick to resent ill treatment. They are revered by those still "fitfully fevering."[26] The greatest number of inhabitants, not given apparently to metaphysical flights up the ladders, search among the throng. Among the crowds are children, but few of them "search." Beckett does note one woman, young but with white hair, holding in her arms "a mite who strains away in an effort to turn its head and look behind" (30)—perhaps an evocation of the Christian mother and child. "None looks within himself where none can be" (30), no "lost one," that is.

The vanquished are "precisely to be counted on the fingers of one hand," says Beckett on page 30, but on the previous page, "cleave also to the wall . . . four vanquished out of five." Are there then four or five vanquished? Ruby Cohn in *Back to Beckett* (258) counts four—the woman with the white hair and the baby, the man stricken rigid in the midst of the fevering (31), and the woman with red hair, and she says we never learn the identity of the fifth. However, if the premise of the metaphysical search as the basis of *The Lost Ones* is correct, perhaps the five are the Platonic, Buddhist, Hindu, Judaic, and Christian metaphysical systems.

Both vanquished and searchers have a long way to go, for in the middle of page 32 Beckett gives the classic description of eternity: "a great heap of sand sheltered from the wind les-

[26]The phrase "fitfully fevering" is drawn from MacBeth, III, 2, l.22. The phrase "the fever of life" is also found in the Anglican *Book of Common Prayer* in the section, "Additional Prayers," in a prayer to be said "At Night," supposed to be the favorite prayer of Cardinal Newman: "O Lord, support us all the day long, until the shadows lengthen and the evening comes, and the busy world is hushed, and the fever of life is over, and our work is done. . . ."

sened by three grains every second year and every following increased by two," a description similar to that by Beckett's friend Joyce in the retreat scene of *A Portrait of the Artist as a Young Man,* a book which also is closely connected with Dante.[27] "In the beginning," Beckett says, using the opening words of the Bible in the King James translation, everyone roamed (searched); now "the faithful," that is, the searchers, are twice as many as the searcher-watchers, who are three times as many as the sedentary who are four times as many as the vanquished who number five in all.

Men and women pause and glance into each other's eyes, but "whatever it is they are searching for it is not that," (36) says Beckett, repeating his own lifelong conviction that love, carnal or romantic, is not the answer to the epistemological quest, echoing not only T. S. Eliot in *The Waste Land,* but Platonic-Christian and most other metaphysics. This comment helps to clear up the early and misleading (probably deliberately so) phrase, "each searching for its lost one" (7), which seems to refer the reader to Plato's myth of sexuality in the *Symposium.* It is characteristic of Beckett to trick the reader in this manner, but whoever the "lost ones" are, they are not lovers.[28]

The effect of the climate on the skin and mucous membranes echoes much of Beckett's early and late Manicheanism, in its emphasis on dryness and dessication and the consequent unpleasant effect on sexual intercourse or "the work of love" (53). For Beckett's characters sexuality has always been more work than love. The dessication of bodies in the cylinder is expressed in physical images which are reminiscent of those used for lust in *A Portrait of the Artist:*

> This dessication of the envelope robs nudity of much of its charm as pink turns grey and transforms into a rustling of nettles the natural succulence of flesh against flesh. (*The Lost Ones,* p. 53)

[27]The original source of this image of the heap of sand is probably the pre-Socratic philosopher, Zeno.

[28]Ruby Cohn states in *Back to Beckett* (257) that the French title of *The Lost Ones, Le Depeupleur,* comes from Lamartine's poem, "L'Isolement," about the loss of a beloved mistress. If true, this source adds irony to Beckett's sardonic view of love.

> A field of stiff weeds and thistles and tufted nettlebunches. Thick among the tufts of rank stiff growth lay battered canisters and clots and coils of solid excrement. A faint marshlight struggled upwards from all the ordure, through the bristling greygreen weeds. (*A Portrait of the Artist*, Viking Critical Edition, p. 137)

Love in the cylinder is a brief madness which astounds even its participants. When the lulls come in the oscillation of light and temperature, the "lovers" are astonished, and "they start to search again neither glad nor even sorry" (55).

A rumor exists in the cylinder that there is a way out. Some have ceased to believe so, but Beckett is at some pains to point out that they are not immune from believing so again (18). There are two chief opinions about the way out: one is that a secret passage or tunnel leads "in the words of the poet to nature's sanctities" (18), an allusion which may be to Francis Thompson's *The Hound of Heaven* (ll. 60–86). The drift is clear: one alternative is to seek the meaning of life in nature or a naturalistic explanation. The other alternative is to dream of "a trapdoor hidden in the hub of the ceiling giving access to a flue at the end of which the sun and other stars would still be shining" (18), an obvious allusion to Dante's Divine Comedy, and thereby possibly to a Christian explanation. "Conversion [a significant word in the context] is frequent either way" (18), yet according to Beckett, the former, or naturalistic view, is declining, albeit extremely slowly, in favor of the Christian alternative (19). Whether the view that the Christian alternative is winning is irony or simply statement of fact, I leave to the sociologists of religion. Those who believe in the tunnel as a way out may be tempted presumably to suicide, whereas the metaphysical view is not susceptible of proof: " . . . the hub of the ceiling is out of reach" (19). The passage on the two ways out concludes with a line in the jeering vein of the younger Beckett, and yet one which exactly poses the ambiguity inherent in all such epistemological dilemmas: "Its fatuous little light will be assuredly the last to leave them *always assuming they are darkward bound*" (*20,* italics mine).

In the arena and inner belt the searchers move at will; in the outer belt, rules of order and precedence strictly prevail.

The rules are such that if a body arrives at the foot of the
ladder and foregoes it, the searcher must then continue
around an entire circuit of the cylinder, or leave the zone and
enter the arena. Thus it is possible that one may never reach
the top of a ladder. However, "the passion to search is such
that no place may be left unsearched" (50–51), and this ur-
gency keeps persistent searchers always waiting in the queues
for the ladders.

The niches are not visible from the floor of the cylinder, and
the climber who does obtain a ladder "relies largely on feel"
when he plants it—presumably an allusion to the intuitive nature of the metaphysical quest. There is, however, one point of
reference or "north": the "woman vanquished." Perhaps this
woman symbolizes the bride of Christ, the one holy Catholic
and Apostolic Church, for she sits with arms and legs crossed,
and she is the north "rather than some other among the vanquished because of her greater fixity" (57). The fact that the
woman has red hair may be significant, red having been traditionally long associated with the church's liturgy and vestments
and with the great feast day of Pentecost when the church, as
such, is said to have begun. The red hair, too, may be an
allusion to the "woman clothed with the sun" in Revelation 12,
who is generally considered by scholars of the Bible to represent the church. Perhaps the greatest tribute paid by Beckett to
the church (along with his descriptions of Sophia Lousse and
the other old women in his trilogy of novels whom I take to
symbolize the church) is the line in *The Lost Ones:* "To one bent
for once on taking his bearings she may be of help" (57), although the remark is so qualified as to become rather faint
praise. Its tone exactly parallels the wry tone of Molloy's comment that in Sophia Lousse's house he at least did not become
worse in health and developed no new ailments.

Some searchers join the climbers simply to study the vanquished, not to find a way out for themselves. In this group we
may subsume all of those academic and sociological students of
religion so characteristic of the twentieth century, who play
with religion and the study of religion as a game rather than
living it as a consecration to a meaningful mystery. Beckett
describes the manner in which many of them study "the
woman vanquished":

> The hair of the woman vanquished has thus many a time been gathered up and drawn back and the head raised and the face laid bare and the whole front of the body down to the crotch. The inspection once completed it is usual to put everything carefully back in place as far as possible. (58)

This description clearly echoes Dante's description of the Siren of Incontinent Worldliness in Canto IX of the *Purgatorio:* "He seized the witch, and with one rip laid bare all of her front, her loins and her foul belly. . . . " One may conclude from this either that Beckett is taking the extreme Protestant view of the Catholic church as the Whore of Babylon, or that belly and crotch are all that such searchers in their reductionist view find in her. However, the former stance would not accord with his statement that "to one bent for once on taking his bearings she may be of help," nor does Beckett's attitude toward the "students" of the vanquished appear to be anything but wryly pejorative. Further, we know that in the famous interview of Beckett by Tom Driver, Beckett pronounced Protestantism "only irksome," and said Catholicism was "deeper." He points out that the "students" do not dare to lay a finger on the watchers waiting in queues for the ladders, for the queues fall violently upon those who dare lay a hand "on the least among them" (Matt. 25:31: "Inasmuch as ye have done it unto one of the least of these my brethren, ye have done it unto me"), a roundabout way of indicating that at least some of the searchers are Christian.

By this time it is apparent that the "lost ones" is an ambiguous term, applying equally to the little people in the cylinder and to those for whom they search so passionately—their lost gods or lost ideals or lost beliefs. The little people are lost, not because they search, but because the lost ones are not found. So life in the cylinder continues until the end of time, when one body is left searching still. Among searchers and vanquished alike, all is motionless. The last searcher "threads his way to that first among the vanquished so often taken for a guide" (62). The context suggests that the "first among the vanquished" is the woman with red hair, or if my surmise is correct, the Catholic church. Thus in *The Lost Ones* the world and the metaphysical search wind down quietly, not with a bang or even with a whimper. The world and the search end, but Beckett has paid his melancholy tribute to the searchers, "one first of whom . . . in some unthinkable past for the first time bowed his head." The knife-edge of ambiguity is maintained right to the end; we do not know if the first searcher bowed his head in reverence—or despair.

IX

The April Morning:
The Purgatorial Quest in *Not I*

God is love . . . she'll be purged

Samuel Beckett

The playlet *Not I* was given its English premiere in London in 1972 and was a stunning success in spite of its brevity and its baffling quality. The first-night audience saw a twelve-minute monologue uttered by the mouth only of a presumably elderly woman. The rest of her was not visible. The Mouth recapitulated her life before a half-seen djellaba-clad auditor, who might have been a psychiatrist, judge, or some other human auditor. Not many one-character plays are written, of whatever length, and the stage-craft of this tiny work, if nothing else, entitles it to notice. Although conflict exists within the mind of the narrator and is deftly projected to the audience, there is no rising action, climax, or denouement. In common with Beckett's longer plays, the work is cyclical, ending where it begins, expressing an eternity of mental torment. Although only one character speaks, a dialogue of sorts is suggested by the narrator's responses to comments or questions unheard by the audience and delivered by a second unseen party, not necessarily by the djellaba-clad figure. Yet the twelve-minute monologue packs an enormous amount of power.

When one has admired the economy of means in *Not I*, one is compelled to ask what the play is saying. Is this a realistic-naturalistic study of a confession to a judge, or to a psychiatrist, or to a priest? Is it a parable of the artist's inability to escape the self and of his/her compulsion to express the self in words, words, words? Or is it, as I believe it is, an almost conventionally religious play about judgment, in a purgatorial existence beyond time?

Keeping in mind Beckett's preoccupation with Good Friday, the crucifixion, the two thieves, and Dante's *Purgatorio*, let us consider what the play says. The Mouth begins by speaking about a newborn child whose father disappeared immediately after her conception and whose mother disappeared immediately after her birth. Presumably this child is herself; she received no parental love as an infant—one of the standard explanations given by psychiatry for an unloving, unfeeling personality. At this juncture the lack of love seems to be the only thing the narrator remembers about her life, up to an episode which happened when she was seventy years old. At this advanced age she was wandering in a field, drifting and staring, looking for cowslips, when suddenly the April light went out, and she found herself in the dark. Whether the dark is death, purgatory, or the dark night of the soul is at this stage of the play unclear. It must be noted, however, that it was an April morning. As has been established already, April is the crucial month in all of Beckett's works, as it was in his life—crucial quite literally, for it is the month of the cross. Good Friday, the day on which Beckett claims he was born, normally occurs in April. Thus immediately after the play establishes the normative modern situation ("I can't love because my parents didn't love me"), it reminds us, however indirectly, of the archvictim of unlovingness and of judgment and redemption.

A second important point is that the voice speaks of herself in the third person, suggesting a certain unwillingness to identify with the actions she is describing. Thirdly, she is apparently corrected in some unseen, off-stage fashion. She insists, as though in reply to a comment, "Who? . . . No! . . . She!" Throughout the monologue this stubborn response to some unheard comment or question is repeated. Although it is obvious that the title, *Not I*, is a disclaimer of responsibility, it is not so obvious that these words are the words of the disciples when confronted by Christ's statement, "One of you that eateth with me shall betray me" (Mark 14:18). In the King James version of the Bible, the disciples answer, "Is it I?" However, the sense of the original Greek, more accurately translated in *The New English Bible* and familiar to all lovers of music from Bach's cantata, is "Not I, surely" (Greek:μητι εγω). Thus, for those who understand it, the play is a picture of judgment and of judgment difficult to divorce from a religious context.

Continuing her description, the woman's voice says that she heard a buzzing, a ray of light came and went; these remind us of a similar humming noise and oscillating light in *The Lost Ones* and also of the light and the "voices" in *The Unnamable*. She does not know what position she was in when the darkness came, but the unseen prompter evidently interrupts and suggests an option she had omitted, for she says, "What . . . kneeling? . . . yes . . . whether standing . . . or sitting . . . or kneeling" (77).

She had been brought up, she says, to believe in a merciful God—and here she laughs heartily, like Mrs. Rooney in *All that Fall*—and her first thought after the light went out was that she was being punished for her sins. Her sins flashed through her mind, but the thought was dismissed when she realized that she was not suffering. The lack of suffering was apparently in contrast to the whole of her previous life, thus arguing for a merciful God after all, although neither she nor the author says so. She has a sudden afterthought—that perhaps she is meant to be suffering, although she is not. Whether she is in hell or purgatory or some other state entirely, her state of being is one in which she herself considers the possibility of confession and of judgment.

The unseen unheard third apparently asks her about the buzzing, and she repeats at greater length the description of the "dull roar in the skull" and the "beam . . . now bright, now shrouded" (78). She implies the light and buzz are intended as torment, but admits again that so far she has suffered no actual pain. Cunningly she thinks it might be well to pretend agony, to writhe and scream, but she can not do so. She does scream on stage, but only to illustrate what she had meant to do and could not do. All is silent, and again the unseen prompter interrupts and she corrects herself: "What? . . . the buzzing . . . yes, . . . all silent but for the buzzing . . . " (79). She was unable to move anything except for her eyelids, but she is not sure even of that. The brain was still active on that April morning, however, and she recalls that she had been hastening toward "a distant bell" (80). Here we are reminded of the gong sounding in the woods to Molloy, and of T. S. Eliot's "reminiscent bells" in *The Waste Land* (l.384).

Shortly thereafter she is corrected by the unseen prompter when she refers to herself in the third person, but *this* suggestion she refuses. Continuing her story, she tells how although her body was still and immovable, she heard a stream of words in her own voice, she who had been silent all her life, even when out shopping in supermarts. She tried to delude herself it was not her voice and almost succeeded, but suddenly had felt her lips and jaw moving and was thus convinced it was herself speaking. She had the awful premonition that all feeling would return to her body, but she was "spared that" (82).

She cannot understand, she says, what she is saying, but she wants to stop saying it. Her brain begs her to stop, but she cannot; her mouth goes on "dragging up the past . . . flashes from all over" (83), remembering mostly her many walks, but also remembering the one time she cried since she was a baby. She was on her way home one evening; but the word "home" is repeated with an exclamation point, in derision, implying it was no real home. On this walk she stopped by a little mound in "Croker's Acres." Beckett's humor is still occasionally juvenile, as in "Croker's Acres"; however, the name may be chosen to make sure that we, the audience, understand the place is a cemetery. Here, without warning, by the "little mound," she wept (83). The little mound is certainly a grave; it may be the grave of someone dear to her, her child perhaps, or it may be "home," her own grave. Once again she is reminded by the unseen prompter of the buzzing. Both the noise and light make it hard for her to think, she says. For a moment she can't go on, or says she can't, then she mutters . . . "God is love . . . she'll be purged . . . " (84) and recalls once again the April morning, the light going out, the whole process of becoming immobile with the voice verbalizing. Once again she refuses to say "I," then she recalls that "long after" it had occurred to her that there was something she had to tell (84). She retells the circumstances of her birth; at least we assume it is her birth, but conceivably it could be the birth of someone else, perhaps even of her own child. She recalls a time when she had to appear in court and was asked what she had to say for herself, "mouth half open as usual . . . waiting to be led away . . . glad of the hand on her arm . . . " (84). Her unseen prompter reminds her: "What? . . . had been? . . . yes . . . something that would tell how it had been . . . how she had lived . . . " (85). How she had lived is "something she didn't know herself," (85), but if she could tell it she would be forgiven. Thus the court may be a literal court in her "real" life, or it may represent divine judgment. She repeats, "God is love," (85) and mutters a phrase from a hymn to which Beckett has alluded in *Malone Dies*. "New every morning" is the phrase she mutters; it is the opening line of Hymn 260 in the *English Hymnal* of 1906. The hymn is by John Keble, one of the leaders of the Tractarian or High Church movement, and was written in 1822. The lines used by Beckett in *Malone Dies* were: "The trivial round, the common task,/ Will furnish all we ought to ask;/ Room to deny ourselves—a road/ To bring us daily nearer God."

Automatically she returns to the same story of the April morning but is interrupted by her prompter, who apparently tells her that what she must tell has "nothing to do with that" (85). She rambles around, trying, supposedly, to hit on what she should tell to be forgiven. Interrupted and kept in line by the prompter, once again for the fourth time she refuses to refer to herself as "I."

She reasserts her general speechlessness since birth but says that once or twice a year, usually in winter, she had an urge to communicate, and then rambles on, her brain separate and viewing the words, so to speak, "something in her begging . . . begging it all to stop," but she keeps on rehearsing the same stuff about the buzzing, the light. For the fifth time she refuses to relinquish the third person, and the curtain comes down as she is repeating once again the description of the April morning, the morning hymn, God is love. . . .

The only movement in the play is that of the djellaba-clad auditor, who may or may not be the unseen prompter. Four times, at each of the denials of identity and responsibility, the robed figure raises its arms from the sides in a gesture of compassion. Visually this gesture might also present a crucifixion image, if the arms are raised to the sides, as Beckett indicates they should be.

Taken together, the "little mound," the something for which to be forgiven, and the appearance in court strongly suggest two of the four last things, death and judgment. It seems to me that *Not I* is a picture of a purgatorial state or a vision of judgment before God. Actually, it may even be a judgment before the Trinity, if I may speculate rather freely: the djellaba-clad figure with its arms outstretched may represent Christ, the unheard prompting voice the Holy Spirit within the soul, and the light and buzzing the godhead or ground of being.

Whether these speculations are too fantastic or not, *Not I* is concerned with the four last things—death, judgment, and (by implication) hell and heaven, i.e., punishment or redemption—themes that have been constant with Beckett ever since the war and *Waiting for Godot,* in which Vladimir and Estragon discuss the possibility of being saved. In the latter play and in the trilogy of novels, *Molloy, Malone Dies,* and *The Unnamable,* these themes are condensed into the image of the two thieves, one of whom was saved, one of whom was damned, while the purgatorial landscape, the light and buzzing in the skull (Golgotha—place of the skull), are constant threads in the above-mentioned works and also in *The Lost Ones* and *Not I.*

Those committed to the view that Beckett is by definition an atheist and nonbeliever in any metaphysical system will declare that *Not I* is ironic and therefore automatically a repudiation of such concepts as judgment and redemption. Yet in *Not I* the irony and the compassion both are almost wholly directed at the unfortunate, fearful, rationalizing human being whose mouth keeps talking, talking, talking, in a futile effort at self-justification. *Her* irony is occasionally directed at God, but to argue that Beckett's is directed against God also is tantamount to saying that the creature is the same as the creator, and to confuse Beckett's irony at his creature's expense with her irony at God.

Not I is the clearest, least ambiguous statement by Beckett on the subject of personal moral responsibility. In *Waiting for Godot,* the trilogy, *Watt,* and *The Lost Ones,* the circumstances of the protagonists are so baffling, so enveloped in mystery and symbolism, that the individual protagonist's responsibility for his own actions, in the eye of God *or* man, is obscured. But in

Not I, the Mouth is clearly justifying herself before a human auditor and, if I interpret correctly the symbolism of the gestures made by this auditor, justifying herself before God. On the basis of *Not I,* it seems that Beckett has presented the drama of the *Purgatorio* or perhaps even the *Inferno* pared down to a twelve-minute recital of sin by a single mouth which refuses to admit personal guilt and responsibility. Beckett's purgatory may not resemble Dante's very much, but it is surely a deadly accurate picture of our modern secularized society and of the plight of many so-called Christians.

X

Naming the Unnamable:
The Quest of the Author

There are many ways in which the thing I am trying in
vain to say may be tried in vain to be said.

Samuel Beckett

How shall I tell of the movements of the soul
in concrete images?

St. Augustine

Must all be veil'd while he that reads divines,
Catching the sense at two removes?

George Herbert

The reader who has come this far may wonder whether Beckett's M–character, his quester, is not actually searching for nothingness, the void, death—just as Esslin and Hassan, for example, say he is. On the other hand, is the mystification with which Beckett's work confronts the reader merely solipsist or elitist obfuscation? Most so-called nihilistic works conceal clues to some norms the writer values, and in the case of Beckett, I find several rhetorical devices which indicate his concerns and scale of values. Foremost among these is his nonstop allusiveness, followed closely by the several uses of Beckettian irony. Less apparent, but equally suggestive, are the settings, the character of the protagonist(s), the resemblances between Beckett's style and content and those of Eliot, Dante, and Langland, and finally, the important question of tone.

To begin with the simplest and most obvious matters, the settings of the works under discussion are nonrealistic and symbolic in the highest degree. Beckett's forest, countryside, road, and garden can be seen as "real" forest, countryside, road, and garden, but they also represent respectively moral confusion (forest), the quest (road and countryside), and the unity and peace of man reconciled to the transcendent (garden), as in Dante, Langland, and Christian tradition generally. Cities in the works are sketchy and nonrealistic; they in no way represent all those grim aspects of modern technology and urban complexity which incline men's hearts to despair. *Watt* begins in a fairly realistic city square, but once Watt gets on the celestial railway and arrives at Mr. Knott's house, all resemblances to literal reality are purely coincidental. In the third part of *Watt*, he and Sam are in what many critics call an institution, thinking perhaps of such well-known and well-established hostelries for the insane as Bedlam and Bellevue. But the place where Sam and Watt talk is not at all like any realistic hospital for the insane; it is purely symbolic of a state of mind. For one thing, each of them has his own garden, a luxury denied most inhabitants of insane asylums or mental hospitals. In *Godot*, we are on a country road in a wastelandish setting with a single tree. *The Lost Ones* may be seen as a kind of city-state, to be sure, but it takes place inside a cylinder and no detail resembles anything like the world around us at time of writing. *Not I* begins in a field in April, but this is obviously a memory of the narrator; the story is taking place inside her head.

The city in *Molloy*, with its walls, watchmen, and slaughterhouse, resembles cities of Biblical or medieval times. The setting of *Malone Dies* is a single room, but it is not the enclosed and recognizably twentieth-century room into which Pinter's characters retreat in terror from overpowering urban rot and technological enslavement. The room in *Malone Dies* has a window from which the protagonist sees (even if he does not always see) the moon, stars, and birds. In the final novel, the *persona* is in a "void," or at any rate he is in no space properly recognizable as space, and there is no "setting" except in his mind, but that one is highly significant. Mahood's jar is situated outside the restaurant near the shambles, where the sunset streams in the firmament like Christ's blood.

The M–quester himself, with his shock of white hair, his shambling gait, his physical infirmities, and his dirty, ragged clothes, is of course the clown-and-tramp figure familiar from circus routines and Chaplin movies—comic enough, if you don't mind laughing at age, sickness, and poverty. In *The Lost Ones* and *Not I*, the questers are more nearly ordinary men and women, although in the former they appear to be unclothed and in the latter the quester is a middle-aged woman. Generally speaking, however, the questers are not wealthy or middle-class. Certainly from the vantage point of a well-fed, well-dressed, affluent reader, the questers strike one as symbols of despair. But suppose they are not? After all, poverty and age and a wandering, hand-to-mouth existence have not at all times and in all places been regarded as an unfortunate and unrewarding way of life.[29] Beckett is known chiefly as an ironist; in this case, suppose the irony is at our expense—we the citizens of the most youth-oriented and most affluent culture in the world?

At any rate, in most of these works we have the strange figure of the thin, poverty-stricken tramp wandering through an unidentifiable landscape, a figure who arouses poetic and mythological echoes. The tramp figure could be based on the Irish tinker-tramp figure, seen frequently in Yeats's work and then identified with the poet or imaginative man. Other artists have written of questers in vague landscapes; three who seem particularly relevant are Eliot, Dante, and Langland. Indeed, looked at in this light, Beckett becomes a part of a great movement of Western literature away from realism and toward symbolic or analogic modes under the sign of Dante—a group in which I find not only Eliot in *The Waste Land*, but earlier, Hawthorne (*The Marble Faun*), and later, Joyce (*A Portrait of the Artist as a Young Man*), and Forster (*A Passage to India*).

The most obvious resemblance between Eliot and Beckett is the technique of literary allusion, but there are many others. Both use shifting "voices" or *personae* and kaleidoscopic mon-

---

[29]An interesting illustration of this is the great French film *La Grande Illusion*, in which two ragged men wander over the countryside. The "Beckettian" flavor of the film is quite striking. We must not forget that Beckett was just such a wanderer during the Occupation, and probably saved his life by fleeing as a tramp.

tages of shifting images. I have noted as they occurred in the trilogy language echoes which recall Eliot's *The Waste Land* and *Four Quartets,* but will briefly recapitulate them: "Here's my beginning" [used to refer to the end of Molloy's life] (Eliot: "In my beginning is my end"); "What shall I do? What shall I do?" (Eliot: "What shall I do now? What shall I ever do?"); "like all recall to life" (Eliot: "April is the cruellest month," "This birth was hard and bitter agony for us,"); the phrase "son of man" (used by Eliot in *The Waste Land); "*instant without bounds" (Eliot: "moment in and out of time"); the reference to the hyacinths in *Malone Dies* (Eliot: "You gave me hyacinths first a year ago"); "I had no wish to arrive, but I had to do my utmost, in order to arrive" (Eliot: "In order to arrive at what you are not/ You must go through the way in which you are not"— paraphrase of St. John of the Cross); "My shadow at evening will not darken the ground" (Eliot: "Or your shadow at evening rising to greet you"); "they want to make a man out of dust" (Eliot: "I will show you fear in a handful of dust"); "They could set a dog on him perhaps, with instructions to drag him out" (Eliot: "Oh keep the Dog far hence, that's friend to man/ Or with his nails he'll dig it up again"); "the soul in its cage" (Eliot: "each in his prison"); and finally the passage too long to quote describing the wasteland (p. 38 above). Lest these verbal echoes be thought suspect because they would not apply to the French versions, we must note resemblances in thought; these include the wasteland ambience, the dependence on Dante, St. Augustine, and the Bible, the emphasis on *akedia* as the central failing of mankind, the concept of the world as a hospital, the disgust with sexuality, the sense of loss and alienation. In addition, the image of the tree and the necessity of patient waiting on God occur in *Murder in the Cathedral.* The form of *Not I,* the agonized, reminiscences of an elderly person, resembles that of *Gerontion.*

Doubtless some of the similarities in phrasing and content are a consequence of the common source in Christian tradition, yet the parallels are striking, and others have been noted by Harvey and Fletcher. Harvey's *Samuel Beckett: Poet and Critic* begins with five pages establishing the connection between Beckett's earliest published poem, *Whoroscope,* and *The Waste Land.* The dense allusiveness of *Whoroscope,* its telescoped images and erudite footnotes, appear to have been modelled on Eliot's poem. Again, according to John Fletcher in his study of Beckett's poetry, the poem *Sanies I* is a pastiche of *Prufrock,* while *Sanies II,* with its repetition of the *kyrie* (also used in *Waiting for Godot),* reveals its kinship to Eliot's *Ash Wednesday. Serena I* is a similar pastiche of the London sections of *The Waste Land.* In *Serena II,* Beckett includes an allusion to *The Tempest,* as he does also in *Endgame*— allusions which would be a matter of indifference were it not that *The Tempest* is one of the parameters underlying *The Waste Land.* The "intolerable wrestle with words and meanings" of which Eliot speaks so movingly in the *Quartets* becomes in Beckett's poems, "the churn of stale words . . . the unalterable whey of words," and eventually is one of his most important themes.

Almost necessarily one would wonder if the influence of Eliot extended to thought content as well as style, but so preconditioned are many critics to their view of Beckett as existentialist, pessimist, and/or atheist that they never pursue the matter farther. Obviously, the spiritual illumination and certainty of *Four Quartets* is not Beckett's, yet it seems to me that Beckett's territory is the same as Eliot's (minus the denominational commitment)—the territory of the lost, fragmented modern world, neither very good nor very bad, indolent and uncommitted, yet uneasily conscious of a missing dimension. At any rate, the influence of Eliot, which began so early in Beckett's artistic career, probably carries considerably more weight than some others, such as those of Rabelais, Sterne, and Swift. It is a tragic irony, perhaps, that Beckett achieved what Eliot hoped to do— to create a new poetic theater, although Beckett's "poetry" is of a different and even less traditional order than Eliot's.

The connections between Beckett and Dante are many and intense, especially in the earlier part of Beckett's career. I have already noted the purgatorial landscape, the centrality of *akedia*—itself the central sin in the *Purgatorio*—and the pivotal role of Belacqua, whose posture appears in *Watt* (33), in the trilogy, and in *The Lost Ones* (14). That the souls of Beckett's protagonists are exiled and alienated does not cancel out the influence of Dante; so are the souls of Dante's protagonists, to a degree. As Dante himself says of the souls in purgatory, they are "exiled children of Eve," or as Eliot says in *Ash Wednesday,* they are "the children at the gate, who will not go away and cannot pray." The souls in the *Purgatorio* walk onwards through stifling smoke and flickering flames, which remind us of the smoke surrounding the charcoal-burner in *Molloy* and the sulphurous flames on the plain in the same work. The landscape of both worlds includes the green wood and glimpses of the stars. The seven deadly sins expiated in the *Purgatorio* are loosely paralleled in *Molloy*. The *Purgatorio* begins on Easter morning, while Easter is the occasion of an absurd and horrific climax to *Malone Dies*—both the *Purgatorio* and *Malone* being the central books of their respective trilogies. A tree is significant in both works, although the tree is far more vital to *Waiting for Godot* than it is in the trilogy, where Moran first pities it, then tears a branch from it. In the *Purgatorio,* there are repeated images of the sheep and the shepherd, as there are in the trilogy.

Throughout the trilogy there are frequent references to worms; similarly there is a reference to worms in the *Purgatorio,* Canto X, l. 121. Of course the common source of both references is Psalm 22, used in the Good Friday liturgy. Purgatory in Dante's *Comedy* is a mountain-city protected by a moat, which reminds one of the walled city approached by Molloy, with the canal around it. In spite of the crowds of sinners, Dante's *Purgatorio* is a lonely place, like Beckett's country. According to Helmut Hatzfield in *American Critical Essays on The Divine Comedy* (Robert J. Clements, ed.): "Solitude and silence are actually a dominant note in the lyricism spread over the mountain-city. . . . This mood is stressed from the outset by the appearance of one old man, Cato, on the wide, vague, and lonely beach (Canto I, l. 31): it is emphasized by the wanderer's feeling entirely lost in the pathless plain (Canto I, ll. 118–120) . . . Sordello's isolated appearance in a complete solitude (Canto VI, l. 59) . . . more deserted than the desert (Canto X, 21); the terrace of the silent blind is, in the livid greenish-gray, terrifyingly lifeless (Canto XIII, l. 7)" (84—85). It will be remembered that both Sordello and Belacqua are mentioned in the early pages of *Molloy*, as Molloy wanders over the countryside.

The conceptual center of the *Divine Comedy* is the incarnation. Similarly, the conceptual center of *Watt* and the trilogy is incarnation—suffering humanity as Christ, literary characters as incarnations of the writer's thought. In *Waiting for Godot,* the protagonists are identified with Christ, as is Molloy. The latter work begins with reference to the incarnation, as has been noted; in the final book of the trilogy, references to the day-spring from on high and to the stable in the last few pages bring the circle round again to the beginning, to the Advent season just before Christmas. Virgil hints at the identity of Dante with Christ ("Blessed be she that bore thee," *Inferno*, Canto VIII), just as Beckett hints at the identity of his protagonists with Christ. In *The Lost Ones*, Beckett refers to Dante (". . . one of his rare wan smiles," p. 14). *The Lost Ones* itself is a cosmology structured in imitation or parody of Dante's, with creatures struggling up ladders to find an opening at the top through which the stars can perhaps be seen. The many references to ladders in Beckett's works correspond to the ascending ridges in purgatory. The tree in *Waiting for Godot* corresponds to the leafless tree in Canto 32, lines 37–60, which breaks into leaf after the appearance of Christ as the Griffon.

So much reliance on Dante's structure and imagery at the very least argues some interest in Dante's metaphysics. But allowing for the vast difference in time and culture, Beckett also resembles Dante stylistically in the tripartite structure of *Watt* and the trilogy, and in the word-play, puns and jokes, the repetition of themes and parallel structures. Thomas Bergin, an outstanding American Dante scholar, notes in the same collection of essays referred to above that the repetition of themes and parallel structures gives the *Comedy* a cumulative effect. As modern examples of such cumulative effect through repetition and parallelism, he offers works by Faulkner and Proust, and might well have included Beckett's *Watt* and the trilogy. In the *Comedy*, for example, the mountain to be climbed in Canto I, *Inferno*, is paralleled by the mountain to be climbed in Canto I, *Purgatorio*. Virgil as guide is paralleled by Beatrice and then by St. Bernard. Francesca is paralleled by Pia; the incident told by Bonconte in *Purgatorio* is paralelled by a similar incident which happened to Bonconte's father, as narrated in the *Inferno*. Similarly, in *Watt*, Arsene's departure and Watt's arrival are paralleled by Watt's departure and Arthur's arrival. In the trilogy, Molloy, Moran, and Mahood each strike and kill someone. In each of the novels of the trilogy, there is a "good" old woman who cares for the protagonist, and in two of the novels there is a hideous old hag who involves the protagonist in sexual intercourse (Ruth-Edith, and Moll). In *Waiting for Godot* the pseudocouple Vladimir-Estragon is paralleled by the pseudocouple Pozzo-Lucky.

Hatzfield claims that the theory of the *Comedy* as didactic allegory has been abandoned, along with the theory of it as a real mystical experience. It is now regarded as "an analogical and implied ascetico-mystical purgation, illumination, and union" (202). Similarly, *Watt* and Beckett's trilogy can each be seen as "an analogical and implied ascetico-mystical purgation and illumination," but without union, without the glorious beatific vision. *Godot* and *The Lost Ones* are metaphoric expressions of the search; *Not I* is a metaphoric expression of the purgatorial state.

On the basis of so much resemblance, especially reinforced by the Eliot parallels, we are, I think, entitled to conjecture that Beckett wishes to give us his version of spiritual quest in modern times, somewhat as Joyce's *Ulysses* both resembles and differs from the *Odyssey* of antique legend.

The vague resemblance of the trilogy to Bunyan's *The Pilgrim's Progress* has been noted by Fletcher (133), but in my view it is only a pale shadow of the resemblance between *Watt* and the trilogy and *Piers the Ploughman*. Other critics have suggested similarities between Eliot and Beckett and between Dante and Beckett, although they have not elaborated to the degree that I have. But no one, so far as I know, has ever suggested any relationship of Beckett's works to *Piers the Ploughman*, probably because in the twentieth century Piers is more often regarded as a Marxist crusader for the underprivileged than as a spiritual quester. But consider the likenesses. As in *Piers*, the questers in *Watt*, the trilogy, and *Godot* are tall and thin, and dressed as beggars. The pilgrims in *Watt* and the trilogy are indolent and accuse themselves in this regard, as does Piers. *Piers the Ploughman* is a series of allegorical dreams described by the narrator, Will, a version of Langland himself, while *Watt's* third portion is described by the narrator, Sam, a version of Beckett himself, and the trilogy is a series of stories told by a fictional narrator who reveals himself in the end to *be* the author. *Piers* follows the liturgical year, while the trilogy does so in a looser and more casual way. As Beckett himself says, "Thus with the year Seasons return" (*Malone Dies*, 33), a seemingly casual quotation from *Paradise Lost* easily passed over unless one notes the context, which is Easter week. The liturgical year in the trilogy begins with the incarnation references in *Molloy* and proceeds through a period of wandering which is perhaps equivalent to Lent. Easter is a climactic moment in both works, although in the trilogy Easter is first a memory and then, in the absurd context of a murderous trip to an island, it is associated with a vision of lights. Approximations of the Crucifixion and of Pentecost hover throughout the three novels, and the trilogy ends with a "soul" waiting to be incarnated, in what one could regard as a kind of Advent season. *Watt* begins in midsummer and ends in summer a year later, while winter, to the sound of chapel bells and church bells, is mentioned during his stay in Knott's house. However, the liturgical references in *Watt* are too vague to approximate the liturgical year.

I have suggested in earlier chapters that many of Beckett's characters resemble the allegorical personifications we find in Langland, such as the characters of Sloth and Gluttony, for example. Just as in *Piers* the Samaritan dissolves into Piers and Piers into the person of Christ, so all Beckett's questers dissolve into each other and all are Christ-figures. The tree which is so prominent a feature of *Waiting for Godot* and which also appears in *Molloy* is a significant image in *Piers the Ploughman*. Most importantly, the pilgrims in *Piers, Godot,* and the trilogy are all concerned with the problem of the two thieves (i.e., salvation). Stylistically, the works share many qualities: the mixture of fantasy and realism, lyricism and harsh coarseness, the vernacular and the erudite, and also repetition and parallelisms.

It would be easy to say that these works of Beckett share the qualities of these three great quest works (*Piers the Ploughman, The Divine Comedy, The Waste Land*) only to mock them, to show with unsparing irony the uselessness and hopelessness of the spiritual quest of modern man. And to be sure, this much is true: Beckett does mock some aspects of popular religion, and there is no beatific vision at the end of Beckett's quest. Watt never encounters Mr. Knott face to face, Godot does not come in person, the "real silence," the "pure plateau" are never achieved, the "Lost Ones" remain lost. However, those facts in themselves do not negate the quest nor the object of the quest, not if we are to believe Beckett's own words, "I can't go on, I'll go on."

The assertion that Beckett is above all a despairing nihilist depends upon which works one is discussing, upon the assumption that the work under discussion is pervaded by unrelieved irony, and in turn upon one's definition of irony. In *The Dry Mock: A Study of Irony in Drama*, Alan Thompson says that irony involves conflicting and incongruous attitudes; it is painful and destructive, yet evokes enough of the ridiculous to make us laugh. This is certainly the common understanding of irony, and of this kind of irony there is plenty in Beckett's trilogy. Yet if one goes carefully through the text, noting the "set pieces" of irony, so to speak, it is noteworthy that none of them is directed against the sense of transcendence, or of that dimension of life inscrutable to reason and science. Occasional sardonic remarks are directed against the popular notion of God or against literal interpretations of religious dogma and practice, particularly in *Watt* and in the Moran section of *Molloy*. However, the most common objects of destructive irony, which by the way falls off sharply in *The Unnamable*, are, in descending order of frequency and importance: the body and its functions, sexual intercourse and consequent generation of children, extreme ratiocinative processes, academic and other bureaucracies, literal and popular notions of religion, and kind, patronizing ladies. With the exception, perhaps, of the kind, patronizing ladies, these objects of irony fall within the classic Christian tradition, as demonstrated by, say, Swift.

But there is another kind of irony, less forceful. As Cleanth Brooks puts it in "Irony as a Principle of Structure" in *Literary Opinion in America*, this irony is "acknowlegement of the pressures of the context." Such irony I will call "indicative irony." In all irony, the opposite of the given statement is present in the mind of the writer and is generally obvious—the body is opposed by the spirit, sexuality by love, reason by intuition, life by death, and so on. In indicative irony, however, the entire context of a work, the frame of reference, the system of values, is intimated but never clearly defined. *Godot, Watt,* and the trilogy, *The Lost Ones* and *Not I* are pervaded by this kind of irony, which is a good deal more subtle and less savage than the irony of such set pieces as the descriptions of Edith or Moll or of Lucky's monologue or of the sucking-stone routine. The strategies subsumed under indicative irony might be summed up as a rhetoric of allusions—in titles, quotations, epigraphs, paraphrases, allegory, parable.

With few exceptions, as we have seen, *Watt*, *Godot*, the trilogy, *The Lost Ones*, and *Not I* either allude to or offer close parallels to the Bible (especially to the New Testament), the Anglican Prayer Book and Hymnal, the *Divine Comedy*, Eliot's *The Waste Land*, *Ash Wednesday*, and *Four Quartets*, Pascal's *Pensées*, Simone Weil's *Waiting for God*, and the poems of George Herbert. The Christian character of these allusions and parallels, when recognized, has been explained away as irony at the expense of Christianity, irony which illustrates the discrepancy between the "near-meaningless, near-despairing lives of the characters and the Judeo-Christian teaching about the human condition," as Mueller and Jacobsen put it in "Samuel Beckett's Long Saturday" (90). But again, suppose it is not irony, as the term is generally understood? Or rather, suppose it is a double-edged, indicative irony, a joke on the secular twentieth century as well as on official Christianity? Suppose that whole other world of grace—the garden of Eden, the City of God, the upper room, the empty tomb—is skillfully evoked by Beckett *for those who are aware of it*, by its seeming negations: Lousse's garden where the dog is buried at the foot of the tree, the railroad station in *Watt* and the city walls in *Molloy*, the room where Malone, alone in bed, sees a vision of fiery lights, the tomb of Mahood in the sealed jar, the blasted tree in *Godot*, the ladders up to the alcoves in *The Lost Ones*, the veiled figure raising its arms in *Not I*?

After all, in what language can a sophisticated twentieth-century writer of wide experience, enormous erudition, and sardonic humor convey a religious quest, or—worse yet—a mystical religious quest? As William Mueller says in the introduction to his *The Prophetic Voice in Modern Fiction:*

> One reason a Dante or a Milton would be unlikely in this century is that the biblical situations and the biblical vocabulary have been so overworked and sentimentalized by superficial and inept artificers that the serious writer struggling with the same basic problems must resort to different situations and different vocabulary. . . . the most profound religious writing is frequently to be found in works which

may initially appear to have little or nothing to do with man's relationship to God. (11)

However, in regard to Beckett, the statement is not such a paradox as it appears. Given the prevailing secularism, Beckett can write about ladders, a tree, narrow wicket gates, shepherds and sheep, knife-rests with two crosses, plumblines and hooks for the soul, veronicas and sudaria, and a weeping single eye, and few persons will recognize the context. If they do, they explain it away as irony. The hiddenness of God in the material world is reflected in the hiddenness of the transcendent in Beckett's writing. Form follows content, indeed. As Lawrence Harvey says, "No one, not Beckett himself, can presume to assay the nature of his relationship to the God who is absent yet everywhere present in his writing" (412).

To others, however, "The constant echo of the New Testament, distorted just sufficiently to make its recognition produce a fresh sense of reality, is omnipresent. Its saturation produces a curiously cumulative effect. Even without the reiterated and overt images of crucifixion and expiation, it provides a magnet to the work's needle, so that we are unable to forget the direction of Beckett's emotional drive." So says Josephine Jacobsen in *The Testament of Samuel Beckett* and she continues, "One might truthfully say that to a reader completely ignorant of the Gospels and the Mass a heavy proportion of Beckett would be totally lost" (19).

The Christian allusiveness, then, is not so much irony at the expense of avowed Christians (although that is present, chiefly in the description of Mr. Spiro whom Watt meets on the train and that of Moran before he sets out on his pilgrimage), it is also irony at the expense of the secular world; the irony serves as a kind of concealment, but to those with eyes to see and ears to hear, it points in the direction of the divine milieu.

Finally and inescapably, Beckett uses the Christian context, as the mountain climbers scale the Himalayas, because it is there. In the Western world it is difficult, if not impossible, to evoke successfully the profoundest questions about man's being and purpose without using the symbolic language of Judeo-Christianity. The insipidity and banality of the symbolism created by newer religions, newer systems of thought and feeling—each reader may color in his own—reveal the impossibility of instant Jungianism, or to put it another way, of creating a new "revelation." Even the systems of Blake and Yeats, geniuses both, have a kind of crankiness or oddity compared to the simplicity, at once homely and majestic, of the Judeo-Christian mythology, which in its turn incorporates images from Greek mythology—the slain god, the wheat and grapes, the libation, the mysteries. Until mankind creates another 2500-year-old religious tradition, the tongues of fire, the wind, the sheep and the shepherd, the dove, the wheat and grapes, and the cross will continue to evoke the deepest possible emotions among those for whom these symbols have, or had, or could have, any meaning.

The aspect of Beckett's style which best supports my thesis (that some of these works analogically represent the negative way and that all are in fact concerned with Christian mysticism and theology) is the tone—a most difficult matter to discuss since one's reactions to tone are inevitably subjective. Nevertheless, I think one can see in the trilogy three distinct tones: first, that of savage destructive irony, directed primarily against the functions of the body and against sexuality; second, a gentler, almost tender or compassionate, indicative irony, which contrasts the hideously fragmented and chaotic, solipsist world of the protagonists with a "norm" which is underground or hidden; and third and last, a lyrical tone which celebrates moments of beauty and union with something or someone, usually in the context of nature. The third tone is often sharpened by a yearning for something more, something grander—but whether this something is intellectual proof or the Beatific Vision itself would be hard to say.

It would be wearying to give a multiplicity of examples of these three tones, particularly since examples of the lyrical tone and the tone of indicative irony are already scattered throughout this study. Below, however, are examples of the three different tones, primarily passages which have not already been quoted in the text:

Tone I (savage, destructive irony):

> So that I would have hesitated to exclaim, with my fingers up my arsehole for example, Jesus-Christ, it's much worse

than yesterday, I can hardly believe it is the same hole. I apologize for having to revert to this lewd orifice, 'tis my muse will have it so. (*Molloy*, 107)

The spectacle was then offered of MacMann trying to bundle his sex into his partner's like a pillow into a pillow-slip, folding it in two and stuffing it in with his fingers. But far from losing heart they warmed to their work. And though both were completely impotent they finally succeeded, summoning to their aid all the resources of the skin, the mucus and the imagination, in striking from their dry and feeble clips a kind of sombre gratification. (*Malone Dies*, 89)

Though we know what we know, said Mr. Spiro, we are not partisan. I personally am a neo-John-Thomist, I make no bones about that. But I do not allow it to stand in the way of my promiscuities. Podex non destra sed sinistra— what pettiness. Our columns are open to suckers of every persuasion and freethinkers figure in our roll of honour. (*Watt*, 28)

This desiccation of the envelope robs nudity of much of its charm as pink turns grey and transforms into a rustling of nettles the natural succulence of flesh against flesh. The mucous membrane itself is affected which would not greatly matter were it not for its hampering effect on the work of love. But even from this point of view no great harm is done so rare is erection in the cylinder. (*The Lost Ones*, 53)

Tone II (indicative irony);

And all sorts of birds. They come and perch on the window-sill, asking for food! It is touching. They rap in the window-pane, with their beaks. I never give them anything. But they still come. What are they waiting for? They are not vultures. (*Malone Dies*, 7)

She is an old woman. I don't know why she is good to me. Yes, let us call it goodness, without quibbling. For her it is certainly goodness. I believe her to be even older than I. But rather less well preserved, in spite of her mobility.

Perhaps she goes with the room, in a manner of speaking. In that case she does not call for separate study, but it is conceivable that she does what she does out of sheer charity, or moved with regard to me by a less general feeling of compassion or affection. Nothing is impossible. I cannot keep denying it much longer. (*Malone Dies*, 8)

The sensations, the premonitions of harmony are irrefragable, of imminent harmony, when all outside him will be he, the flowers the flowers that he is among him, the sky that is above him, the earth trodden the earth treading, and all sound his echo. When in a word he will be in his midst at last, after so many tedious years spent clinging to the perimeter. (*Watt*, 40–41)

At me too someone is looking, of me too someone is saying, He is sleeping, he knows nothing, let him sleep on. (*Waiting for Godot*, 58a)

One school swears by a secret passage branching from one of the tunnels and leading in the words of the poet to nature's sanctuaries. The other dreams of a trapdoor hidden in the hub of the ceiling giving access to a flue at the end of which the sun and other stars would still be shining. (*The Lost Ones*, 19)

Tone III (lyrical and/or yearning):

He hears, that's all about it, he who is alone and mute, lost in the smoke, it is not real smoke, there is no fire, no matter, strange hell that has no heating, no denizens, perhaps it's paradise, perhaps it's the light of paradise, and the solitude, and this voice the voice of the blest interceding invisible, for the living, for the dead, all is possible. (*The Unnamable*, 100)

And I can even distinctly remember the paper-hangings or wallpaper still clinging in places to the walls and covered with a writhing mass of roses, violets, and other flowers in such profusion that it seemed to me I had never seen so many in the whole course of my life, nor of such beauty.... And during all this time, so fertile in incidents and mishaps, in my head I suppose all was streaming and emptying away as through a sluice, to my great joy, until nothing remained, either of Malone or of the other. (*Malone Dies*, 49–50)

And then another night fall and another man come and Watt go, Watt who is now come, for the coming is in the shadow of the going and the going is in the shadow of the coming, that is the annoying part about it. And yet there is one who neither comes nor goes, I refer I need hardly say to my late employer, but seems to abide in his place, for the time being at any rate, like an oak, an elm, a beech or an ash, to mention only the oak, the elm, the beech and the ash, and we nest a little while in his branches. (*Watt*, 57)

VLADIMIR: To have lived is not enough for them.
ESTRAGON: They have to talk about it.
VLADIMIR: To be dead is not enough for them.
ESTRAGON: It is not sufficient.
                      Silence
VLADIMIR: They make a noise like feathers.
ESTRAGON: Like leaves.
VLADIMIR: Like ashes.
ESTRAGON: Like leaves.   (*Waiting for Godot*, 40 A)

And far from being able to imagine their last state when every body will be still and every eye vacant they will come to it unwitting and be so unawares. Then light and climate will be changed in a way impossible to foretell. (*The Lost Ones*, 15)

God is love . . . tender mercies . . . new every morning . . . back in the field . . . April morning . . . face in the grass . . . nothing but the larks . . . pick it up—(*First Love and Other Shorts*, 87)

Needless to say, these quotations are intended only as samples; the best proof of any generalizations about a writer's style is the entire work itself. I am confident that these three tones (and perhaps others) are generally to be found in the works under discussion and that their artistic purpose is related to the conveying of something other than despair or nihilism.

One who accepts the view of these works as analogues of the

negative way of mysticism in modern times will have no difficulty in seeing why the outcome is necessarily frustrated, or at
best, in doubt. Given the secular materialism of our culture, its
worship of science and technology, its fragmentation and alienation from sources of passion and intuition, the terrible weak-
nesses of its churches, it is almost inevitable that intelligent,
sensitive men will find their way to the transcendent blocked at
every turn. But the protagonists of the trilogy (and also of *Watt,
Godot, The Lost Ones,* and *Not I*) appear to have special problems
which may or may not be common to other persons of our
time: a dissociation from and disgust with sexuality and the
other functions of the body, along with an accompanying deep-
rooted concupiscence, a moral apathy, a torpid indolence, and
finally, simply, a lack of love. Other than the compassion shown
occasionally by the writer for his creatures, by Sam for Watt,
for instance, by Vladimir for Estragon and by the three shadowy females, one in each book of the trilogy, who nurture the
protagonists, there is no love in these works. Whether they are
microcosms of the world of today or not, this is the most damn-
ing of all the indictments offered by Beckett. Even that mud-
dled mystic, Rimbaud, who said, "J'attends Dieu avec gourman-
dise" (Zaehner, *Mysticism: Sacred and Profane,* 69), eventually
realized he was on the wrong track: "I thought of seeking out
again the key to the ancient feast at which, perhaps, I might
recover my appetite. Charity is the key" (Zaehner, 69). Beckett
is certainly aware that charity is the key, but in the closed,
solipsist world of his creations there is little love, only murderous or lustful impulses which alternate with periods of apathy
and periods of yearning and searching for the real silence, the
pure plateau. Yet the search goes on. Like Pascal, Beckett "can
only commend those who search with groans" (*Pensée* 333).

Although the 1969 Nobel Prize Committee called Beckett's
work a *dies irae* of the human race, certainly an applicable term,
it might more justly be regarded as a *miserere,* as suggested by
Dr. Karl Gierow of the Swedish Academy in its official statement: "In the realm of annihilation, the writing of Samuel
Beckett rises like a *miserere* from all mankind, its muffled minor
key sounding liberation to the oppressed and comfort to those
in need" (*New York Times,* October 24, 1969, p. 32). Significantly, the *miserere* occurs in the *Purgatorio* immediately after

Dante's encounter with Belacqua. The *miserere* is based on Psalm 51, which begins, "Have mercy upon me, O God, according to thy lovingkindness," and includes the relevant verses, "Behold I was shapen in iniquity; and in sin did my mother conceive me," and "Cast me not away from thy presence; and take not thy holy spirit from me."

What Beckett would make of this explication of some of his works is not easy to imagine—a diffident Irish smile, probably. But we must trust the tales and not the teller, especially not such a disingenuous teller. The tales will frequently reveal much the teller would never admit in public. In the works named, hints and guesses at perfection fall like gentle, irregular rain in a dry place. And if one is to believe what Beckett says in *The Lost Ones*, the searcher "by feeble fits and starts is searching still."

Bibliography

Adams, Robert. *Nil: Episodes in the Literary Conquest of Void During the Nineteenth Century.* New York: Oxford University Press, 1966.

Augustine, Saint. *Confessions,* trans. Edward B. Pusey. New York: Collier, 1961.

Baeck, Leo. *Judaism and Christianity,* trans. and introd., Walter Kaufman. New York: The World Publishing Company, and Philadelphia: The Jewish Publication Society, 1958.

Bair, Deirdre. *Samuel Beckett: A Biography.* New York: Harcourt Brace Jovanovich, 1978.

Baldwin, Hélène. "The Theme of the Pilgrim in the Works of Samuel Beckett," *Christian Scholar's Review,* vol. VIII, no. 3, pp. 217–227.

Barnard, G. C. *Samuel Beckett: A New Approach. A Study of the Novels and Plays.* New York: Dodd, Mead and Co., 1970.

Beckett, Samuel. *Endgame.* New York: Grove Press, 1958.

——. *First Love and Other Shorts.* New York: Grove Press, 1974.

——. *Happy Days.* New York: Grove Press, 1961.

——. *How It Is.* New York: Grove Press, 1964.

——. *Krapp's Last Tape.* New York: Grove Press, 1958.

——. *The Lost Ones.* New York: Grove Press, 1972.

——. *Malone Dies.* New York: Grove Press, 1956.

——. *Molloy.* New York: Grove Press, 1955.

——. *More Pricks Than Kicks.* New York: Grove Press, 1972.

——. *Not I.* New York: Grove Press, 1974.

——. *Poems in English.* New York: Grove Press, 1961.

——. *Proust.* New York: Grove Press, 1957.

——. *Stories and Texts for Nothing.* New York: Grove Press, 1967.

——. *The Unnamable.* New York: Grove Press, 1958.

——. *Waiting for Godot.* New York: Grove Press, 1954.

——. *Watt.* New York: Grove Press, 1959.

Bergin, Thomas. *Perspectives on the Divine Comedy.* New Brunswick, N.J.: Rutgers University Press, 1967.

Boethius. *The Consolation of Philosophy*, trans. Richard Green. New York: Bobbs-Merrill, 1962.

Bonhoeffer, Dietrich. *Letters and Papers from Prison*. New York: Mac-Millan, 1953.

Book of Common Prayer of the Protestant Episcopal Church in the United States of America. New York: Harper and Brothers, 1940.

Booth, Wayne. *The Rhetoric of Fiction*. Chicago: Chicago University Press, 1961.

Boros, Ladislas. *The Hidden God*. New York: Seabury Press, 1973.

Brion, Marcel. *Romantic Art*. New York: McGraw Hill, 1960.

Brooks, Cleanth. "Irony As a Principle of Structure," in *Literary Opinion in America*, ed. Morton Dauwen Zaubel. New York: Harper and Brothers, 1937.

Brown, John Russell, ed. *Modern British Dramatists: A Collection of Critical Essays*. Englewood Cliffs, N.J.: Prentice-Hall, 1968.

Browne, Sir Thomas. *Religio Medici and Other Writings*, introd. Frank L. Huntley. New York: Dutton, 1951. Everyman's Library edition.

Bunyan, John. *The Pilgrim's Progress*, introd. and notes, G. B. Harrison. London: J. M. Dent and Sons, 1954.

Butler, Dom Cuthbert. *Western Mysticism*. London: Constable and Co., 1951.

Cabaud, Jacques. *Simone Weil: A Fellowship of Love*. New York: Channel Press, 1964.

Calder, John. *Beckett at Sixty: A Festschrift*. London: Calder and Boyars, 1967.

Campbell, Joseph. *Myths to Live By*. New York: Viking Press, 1972.

Ciardi, John, trans. *Dante Alighieri: The Purgatorio*. New York: New American Library, 1957.

Clements, Robert J., ed. *American Critical Essays on the Divine Comedy*. New York: New York University, 1967.

Cohen, Robert. "Parallels and the Possibility of Influence Between Simone Weil's *Waiting for God* and Samuel Beckett's *Waiting for Godot*." Modern Drama, VI, Feb. 1964, pp. 425–35.

Cohn, Ruby. *Back to Beckett*. Princeton, N.J.: Princeton University Press, 1973.

———. *Samuel Beckett: The Comic Gamut*. New Brunswick, N.J.: Rutgers University Press, 1962.

———, ed. *Casebook on Waiting for Godot*. New York: Grove Press, Inc., 1967.

Driver, Tom. "Beckett by the Madeleine," *Columbia University Forum*, Summer, 1961.

———. *Romantic Quest and Modern Query: A History of the Modern Theater*. New York: Dell, 1970.

Duckworth, Cohn. *Angels of Darkness: Dramatic Effect in Samuel Beckett with Special Reference to Eugene Ionesco*. New York: Barnes and Noble Books, 1972.

Eliot, T.S. *The Complete Poems and Plays*. New York: Harcourt, Brace and World, 1952.

―――. *Selected Essays,* new ed. New York: Harcourt, Brace and World, 1950.

Ellmann, Richard, ed. *The Letters of James Joyce,* Vol. 3. New York: Viking Press, 1966.

The English Hymnal with Tunes. Oxford: Oxford University Press, 1906.

Esslin, Martin, ed. *Samuel Beckett: A Collection of Critical Essays*. Englewood Cliffs, N.J.: Prentice-Hall, 1965.

―――. *The Theatre of the Absurd*. Garden City, N.Y.: Doubleday, 1961.

"Eugene Ionesco Interviewed by Gabriel Jacobs," *Critical Inquiry,* 1, No. 3 (March, 1975), 643.

Everyman, Amersham, England: John S. Farmer, 1913.

Federman, Raymond. *Journey to Chaos: Samuel Beckett's Early Fiction*. Berkeley and Los Angeles: University of California Press, 1965.

Ferguson, George. *Signs and Symbols in Christian Art*. New York: Oxford University Press, 1961.

Fletcher, John. *The Novels of Samuel Beckett*. London: Chatto and Windus, 1967.

―――. *Samuel Beckett's Art*. London: Chatto and Windus, 1967.

Hamilton, Kenneth and Alice. *Condemned to Life: The World of Samuel Beckett*. Grand Rapids, Mich.: Eerdmans, 1976.

Happold, F.C. *Mysticism: A Study and an Anthology*. Baltimore: Penguin, 1967.

Harvey, Lawrence E. *Samuel Beckett: Poet and Critic*. Princeton, N.J.: Princeton University Press, 1970.

Hassan, Ihab. *The Literature of Silence: Henry Miller and Samuel Beckett*. New York: Alfred A. Knopf, 1967.

Herman, E. *The Meaning and Value of Mysticism*. 2nd. ed. London: James Clarke and Co., 1916.

Hesla, David H. *The Shape of Chaos: An Interpretation of the Art of Samuel Beckett*. Minneapolis: University of Minnesota Press, 1971.

Hitchcock, Roswell D. *Hitchcock's Topical Bible and Cruden's Concordance*. Grand Rapids, Michigan, 1952.

Hoffman, Frederick J. *Samuel Beckett: The Language of Self*. Carbondale: Southern Illinois University Press, 1962.

Hymnal of the Protestant Episcopal Church in the United States of America. New York: Harper and Brothers, 1940.

Inge, Dean William Ralph. *Studies of English Mystics*. Freeport, N.Y.: Books for Libraries Press, 1969.

The Interpreter's Dictionary of the Bible. ed. George Arthur Buttrick et al. Nashville, Tenn.: Abingdon Press, 1962.

Jacobsen, Josephine, and William Mueller. "Samuel Beckett's Long Saturday" in *Man and the Modern Theater,* ed. Nathan A. Scott, Jr. Richmond, Va.: John Knox Press, 1965.

―――. *The Testament of Samuel Beckett*. New York: Hill and Wang, 1964.

BIBLIOGRAPHY

The Jewish Encyclopedia, ed. Isidore Singer et al. New York: Ktav Publishing House, n.d.

Joyce, James. *A Portrait of the Artist as a Young Man,* ed. Chester G. Anderson. New York: Viking Press, 1968. Viking Critical Library Edition.

Joyce, Stanlislaus. *My Brother's Keeper: James Joyce's Early Years,* ed. with introd. and notes by Richard Ellmann and preface by T.S. Eliot. New York: Viking Press, 1958.

Juliana of Norwich. *Revelations of Divine Love,* trans. and introd. Clifton Wolters. Baltimore: Penguin, 1966.

Kenner, Hugh. *Samuel Beckett: A Critical Study.* New edition with a supplementary chapter. Berkeley, Calif.: University of California Press, 1968.

Kennedy, Sighle. *Murphy's Bed: A Study of Real Sources and Sur-Real Associations in Samuel Beckett's First Novel.* Lewisburg: Bucknell University Press, 1971.

Langland, William. *Piers the Ploughman,* trans. J. F. Goodridge. Baltimore: Penguin, 1959.

Laurence, Brother. *Letters and Conversations on the Practice of the Presence of God.* Forward Movement edition, n.d.

Leclerq, Jean. *The Love of Learning and the Desire for God: A Study of Monastic Culture,* trans. Catharine Misrahi. New York: New American Library, 1962.

Levy, Alan. "The Long Wait for Godot." *Theatre Arts,* XL (August, 1956), N. 8.

Lietzman, Hans. *A History of the Early Church.* Cleveland, Ohio: World Publishing Co., 1961.

Martz, Louis L. *The Paradise Within: Studies in Vaughan, Traherne, and Milton.* New Haven: Yale University Press, 1964.

Mill, Jan. *Pascal and Theology.* Baltimore: Johns Hopkins, 1969.

Mueller, William R. *The Prophetic Voice in Modern Fiction.* New York: Doubleday, 1959.

Musa, Mark, ed. *Essays on Dante.* Bloomington, Ind.: Indiana University Press, 1964.

The New English Bible. Cambridge: Cambridge University Press, 1961.

New Theatre Magazine. Samuel Beckett Special Issue, XI, No. 3, n.d.

O'Brien, Elmer. *Varieties of Mystic Experience: An Anthology and Interpretation.* New York: New American Library, 1965.

Otto, Rudolph. *The Idea of the Holy: an Inquiry into the Non-rational Factor in the Idea of the Divine and Its Relation to the Rational,* trans. John W. Harvey. 2nd ed. New York: Oxford University Press, 1950.

The Oxford Dictionary of the Christian Church. London: Oxford University Press, 1974.

The Oxford Dictionary of English Etymology. Oxford: Oxford University Press, 1966.

Bibliography

Pascal, Blaise. *The Pensées*, trans. J. M. Cohen. Baltimore: Penguin, 1961.

Pilling, John. *Samuel Beckett*. London: Routledge and Kegan Paul, 1976.

The Poems of George Herbert, introd. Helen Gardner. 2nd ed. London: Oxford University Press, 1961.

The Protestant Mystics, ed. Anne Fremantle, introd. W. H. Auden. Boston: Little, Brown and Co., 1964.

Rees, Richard. *Simone Weil: A Sketch for a Portrait*. Carbondale: Southern Illinois University Press, 1968.

Samuel Beckett Now, ed. Melvin J. Friedman. Chicago: University of Chicago Press, 1972.

Schneider, Alan. "Waiting for Beckett," *Chelsea Review*, No. 2, 1958.

Scott, Nathan, ed. *Man in the Modern Theatre*. Richmond, Va.: John Knox Press, 1967.

The Shorter Oxford English Dictionary. Oxford: Oxford University Press, 1933.

States, Bert O. *The Shape of Paradox: An Essay on Waiting for Godot*. Berkeley: University of California Press, 1978.

Theatre Arts Magazine, XL (August, 1956), pp. 33–35, 95–96.

Thilly, Frank. *A History of Philosophy*, rev. Ledger Wood. New York: Holt, Rinehart and Winston, 1966.

Thompson, Alan W. *The Dry Mock: A Study of Irony in Drama*. Berkeley: University of California Press, 1948.

Thompson, Francis. *Complete Poetical Works*. New York: Boni and Liveright, n.d. Modern Library Edition.

Tillich, Paul. *The Shaking of the Foundations*. New York: Scribner, 1968.

Transition, 16–17, June 1929, pp. 268–271.

Unger, Leonard. "T.S. Eliot's Images of Awareness," in *T. S. Eliot: The Man and His Work*, ed. Allen Tate. New York: Dell, 1968.

Watts, Alan W. *Myth and Ritual in Christianity*. New York: Grove Press, 1960.

Webb, Eugene. *Samuel Beckett: A Study of His Novels*. Seattle: University of Washington Press, 1973.

————. *The Plays of Samuel Beckett*. Seattle: University of Washington Press, 1972.

Webner [Baldwin], Hélène L. "*Waiting for Godot* and the New Theology," *Renascence*, XXI (Autumn, 1968), 3–9, 31.

Weil, Simone. *Waiting for God*, trans. Emma Craufurd. New York: Harper and Row, 1973.

West, Paul. "Hell or Heaven?" *The Washington Post*, Dec. 24, 1972.

Young, Robert. *Young's Analytical Concordance to the Bible*. Grand Rapids: Eerdmans, 1972.

Zaehner, R. C. *Mysticism, Sacred and Profane: An Inquiry into Some Varieties of Praeternatural Experience*. New York: Oxford University Press, 1961.

Index

akedia: Arsene's sin, 94, 95; Belacqua's sin, 30; central sin in *Purgatorio* and *The Waste Land*, 20, 21
Athanasius, St. (c. 293–373), 77
Auden, W.H. (1907–1973), 33
Augustine, St. (354–430), 15, 43, 79; Beckett on, 12; on God, 60, 70; on mysticism, 16, 84, 85; on "two thieves," 44

Basil the Great, St. (329–379), 71
Beckett, Samuel (1906–): and St. Augustine, 10, 12, 26, 27; view of Christ, 33, 62, 63, 76; cross and, 12, 34, 35, 108, 129, 157; and Dante, 10, 26, 27, 147–50; and Descartes, 10, 26, 27; and Eliot, 10, 143–47; French language and, 14; and Geulincx, 26, 27; importance of Good Friday and Easter to, 35, 58, 75n, 78, 98, 109, 137; irony in, 152–53; and Johnson, 88, 89; and Joyce, 10, 143–45; and Langland, 143–45, 150–51; Manicheanism of, 8, 13, 14, 42, 65, 98, 131, 132; and mysticism, 3–5, 20, 24, 26; and Nobel Prize, 2, 159; and Pascal, 26, 27; phases in style of, 9, 90; on religion, 11, 12, 13, 54, 151, 152; satire in, 91, 100, 122, 131; tone in, 155–58; and "two thieves," 44, 108, 122
bells and gongs, 46, 101, 139; angelus, 31
Boehme, Jacob (1575–1624), 70
Bonhoeffer, Dietrich (1906–1945), 123, 124
Boetheus (c. 480–c. 524), 63, 127
Book of Common Prayer, 7; Benedictus, 82; Gloria Patri, 101; Kyrie, 113, 121; marriage service, 104; prayer of Cardinal Newman, 130, 154

Catherine of Genoa, St. (1447–1510), 76
Christ: Beckett characters as figures of, 63, 76, 88, 89, 91, 92, 97, 102; cross and crucifixion of, 34, 35, 50, 76, 108, 109, 114, 137, 140–41; and Golgotha, 117, 141; as Good Shepherd, 49; and Holy Week, 110, 111; and Judas, 48; and Mary and Martha, 48, 95;

resurrection of, 53, 61, 66, 111; as scapegoat, 105; as Son of Man, 62; as suffering humanity, 33, 62, 63, 76, 148
color: red, symbolizing church, 91, 92; gold, white, and blue, 97; woman with red hair, 133, 134

Dante (Dante Alighieri, 1265–1321), 2, 7, 43, 65, 77, 125, 143, 144, 153; Arnaut Daniel, 30; Belacqua, 30, 31, 91, 129, 148; *Divine Comedy*, symbolism in, 59, 80n, 87, 92, 109, 110, 132; forests and trees in, 46, 59, 109, 110, 114; *Inferno*, 49, 50; Mount of Purgatory, 31, 67; *Paradiso*, 54; *Purgatorio*, 30, 31, 35n, 42, 43, 45, 46, 49, 50, 80n, 159, 160; questers in, 87, 145; resemblances to Beckett's work, 125, 126, 128, 147–50; Siren of Worldliness, 42, 133
Democritus (c. 460–c. 370 B.C.), 6, 7

Eckhart, Meister (c. 1260–c. 1329), 24, 60, 69, 70
Eliot, T.S. (1888–1965), 2, 7, 9, 10, 13, 28, 42, 74, 129, 143, 145; *Ash Wednesday*, 93; and Beckett, resemblances in works, 145–47, 153; *Burnt Norton*, 38, 69, 94; *Choruses from "The Rock,"* 67; dark night of the soul and, 22, 69, 76; *Dry Salvages*, 89; *East Coker*, 28, 74, 90; *Four Quartets* (listed under individual poem titles); *Little Gidding*, 21n, 26, 87; *Murder in the Cathedral*, 71–72; *The Waste Land*, 30, 32, 39, 42, 63, 66, 73, 77, 79, 81–82, 131
Eucharist, or Holy Communion, 77; and ambry, 100; analogues to, 34, 98–100; institution of, 111; Knott's meal as, 99–100; and piscina, 98; as viaticum, 67

Fraser, G.S., 4
Fraser, Sir James (1854–1941), 66

Gaber, variant of Gabriel, 47
gate, strait or wicket: Alan Watts on, 59; in New Testament, 43; in *Piers the Ploughman, Pilgrim's Progress*, etc., 43, 92
Geulincx, Arnold (1624–1669), 6, 7, 40; Rudolph Otto on, 40, 53
God, 11, 30, 39, 44, 49, 59, 64, 67, 69, 122, 126, 152, 153; and Adam, 108; anthropomorphizing of, 54, 121; as artist-creator, 69; Beckett's view of, 12, 13; as center and circumference, 70, 93, 101; as commutator, 128; covenant with, 119; as creator of forms, 60; allowing cruelty, 102; defined by negatives, 36–38; as *deus mobilis*, 116; as ethical norm, 111; free will under, 116, 117; Godot as, 107; hand of, 62; hiddenness or absence of, 115, 154; in human form, 124; irony against, 37, 141; judgment before, 141, 142; Knott as, 98; as light, 127; as love, 139, 140, 158; as merciful, 138; mysticism and, 16–27; Obidil as, 52, 53; omnipotence of, 40; prayer to, 116; as savior, 121; as servant, 123; as Trinity, 103, 141; as unnamable, 68; waiting for (on), 41, 58, 63, 115, 119, 122, 146, witnessing to, 104; Youdi as, 47
Gregory, St. (540–604), 19, 20, 63

Virgil (70–19 B.C.), 88

Watt, 20, 21, 23, 24, 86–106 (chapter VI)
Waiting for Godot, 21, 23, 24, 107–124 (chapter VII)
Weil, Simone (1909–1943): on attention, 29; Backett and, 10, 11; as
    Christian mystic, 11; on God, 24, 29, 47, 70, 116; on man, 41, 74;
    on silence, 24, 80n, 83; on "two thieves," 41, 44; *Waiting for God,*
    29, 34; *Waiting for Godot* and, 11n, 107, 153
Wittgenstein, Ludwig (1889–1951), 94